25 Bicycle Tours in
Lake Champlain Region

25 Bicycle Tours in the Lake Champlain Region

CHARLES HANSEN

Scenic Rides
in Vermont,
New York,
and Quebec

 Backcountry Guides
Woodstock, Vermont

First Edition

An Invitation to the Reader
Although it is unlikely that the roads you cycle on these tours will change
much with time, some road signs, landmarks, and other items may. If you find
that such changes have occurred on these routes, please let the author and
publisher know, so that corrections may be made in future editions. Other com-
ments and suggestions are also welcome. Address all correspondence to: Editor,
Backroad Bicycling Series, Backcountry Guides, P.O. Box 748, Woodstock, VT
05091.

Library of Congress Cataloging-in-Publication Data
Hansen, Charles, 1946–
    25 bicycle tours in the Lake Champlain region : scenic rides in Vermont,
New York, and Quebec / Charles Hansen. — 1st ed.
        p. cm.
    ISBN 0-88150-575-7
    1. Bicycle touring—Champlain, Lake, Region—Guidebooks. 2. Champlain,
Lake, Region—Guidebooks. I. Title: Twenty-five bicycle tours in the Lake
Champlain region. II. Title.
    GV1045.5.C53H36 2004
    796.6'4'0974754—dc22   2004046136

Cover and interior design by Bodenweber Design
Composition by Chelsea Cloeter
Maps by Moore Creative Designs © The Countryman Press
Cover photograph by Carolyn Bates courtesy of Lake Champlain
Bikeways, www.champlainbikeways.com
Interior photographs by the author

Published by Backcountry Guides, a division of The Countryman Press, P.O.
Box 748, Woodstock, Vermont 05091

Distributed by W.W. Norton & Company, Inc., 500 Fifth Avenue, New York, NY
10110

Printed in the United States of America

10 9 8 7 6 5 4 3 2 1

This book is dedicated to my parents,
Dorothy and Homer Hansen,
who are responsible for my being on a bicycle today.

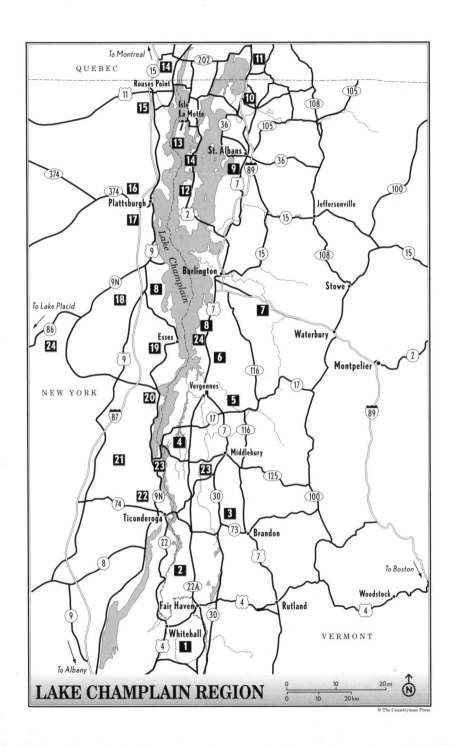

LAKE CHAMPLAIN REGION

© The Countryman Press

CONTENTS

PREFACE Actually, my parents were responsible for my being on a bicycle even before I was born. The family legend is that when they got married my father told my mother that they would have grand adventures together, and she later challenged him with, "Well, let's have one!" In the spring of 1946 they set out from San Diego on three-speed bicycles, using racks and panniers designed and built by my father using lightweight aircraft aluminum and ripstop nylon.

By Labor Day they had reached New York City and I was born three months later, with my mother claiming she was not aware she was pregnant when they started the journey. They have many stories from their trip, and my brother and I grew up seeing the slides that my father shot. He had also printed his own postcards before the expedition, with a depiction of them on their bicycles and the proposed route drawn on a map of the country. Their current location would be indicated on the map when they wrote a card for a family member or friend.

When my brother and I were quite young my father built bicycle seats for us and we would ride everywhere around the city, including weekend picnics on Staten Island with cycling friends of my parents. My father submitted a photo story to the *New York Daily News* that published it under the heading, "A Bicycle Built for One and a Half"; neighbors in our Lower East Side neighborhood couldn't believe that he actually got paid for having his picture in the paper. I have early memories of family hostel trips along the Horseshoe Trail in eastern Pennsylvania, cycling on back roads that roughly followed the equestrian trail. Later my brother and I would ride our own bikes on these annual excursions.

At a fairly young age I was allowed to ride around Manhattan on my own. I took my first solo bike camping tour while in high school. I remember being awakened one Saturday morning by local kids informing me that I had set up my tent in the middle of their baseball diamond the previous night. I hastily dressed, packed the tent and sleeping bag, and returned the field to its rightful owners.

There have been periods in my life when I did not spend much time on a bicycle, but it has always been something that I came back to and I thank my parents for that, as it has made my life richer than it would otherwise be.

ACKNOWLEDGMENTS I would like to thank Anna Panszczyk for her support, patience, flexibility, and tolerance; also for loaning me the Jeepie for a scouting trip when the Vikingmobile was ailing.

For answering my many questions about his experience in having his first book published, and for continuing guidance while I wrote mine, I would like to thank my brother Eric Hansen.

My thanks to Steve Barrett for test riding Tour 9 and for his excellent feedback.

My admiration and gratitude are extended to Agnes Cornelius, who spent part of a pleasant summer afternoon discussing her stone wall restoration and other rock works with me, and for giving permission for riders to explore this amazing work on her property.

My appreciation goes to Richard Fumosa and the entire crew at The Countryman Press for creating such a handsome production of my first book.

TOURS AT A GLANCE

TOUR	REGION	TERRAIN
1. Whitehall–Fair Haven	South	Moderately to seriously rolling; flat on US 7
2. Whitehall–Ticonderoga	South	Gently to seriously rolling
3. Middlebury–Brandon	Vermont Southern	Lightly to moderately rolling; one steep .5-mile climb
4. Middlebury–Vergennes	Vermont Southern	Lightly to moderately rolling
5. Middlebury–Burlington	Vermont Southern	Lightly to moderately rolling; some steeper climbs
6. Charlotte loops	Vermont Central	Lightly rolling (15); moderately rolling
7. Richmond–Hinesburg	Vermont Central	Lightly rolling; some steeper climbs
8. Burlington–Essex	Vermont Central	Moderately rolling
9. Milton–St. Albans	Vermont Northern; Quebec	Flat to lightly rolling; a few steeper sections
10. Swanton–Philipsburg	Vermont Northern; Quebec	Lightly rolling; a few steeper sections
11. Bedford–Philipsburg	Vermont Northern; Quebec	Lightly rolling
12. South Hero loop	Lake Champlain Islands	Flat to lightly rolling
13. Isle La Motte	Lake Champlain Islands	Flat

DISTANCE	DIFFICULTY	HIGHLIGHTS
23 or 32 miles	Moderate to difficult	Rolling quiet roads; Fair Haven; Liberty Hill Animal Land Zoo
57 miles	Moderate to difficult	Dramatic rolling countryside; Fort Ticonderoga; cable ferry; Ticonderoga Heritage Museum
39 or 56 miles	Moderate	Lake Dunmore; Brandon; rolling farmland; mountain and lake views
49 or 62 miles	Moderate	Adirondack views; lakeside riding; Vergennes; Morgan Horse Farm
65 or 86 miles	Moderate (86 over 2 days); moderate to difficult (65 in 1 day)	Long day loop or overnight trip to Burlington; Bristol; Green Mountain views; Burlington bike path; Vergennes
15, 25, 34, or 42 miles	Easy (15); moderate to difficult	Charlotte; rolling roads in farm country; Vergennes (34/42); Mount Philo (optional climb and view)
30 miles	Moderate	Views of Camel's Hump and Mount Mansfield; quiet river-valley riding; historic Old Round Church
42 or 50 miles	Moderate	Ride in 2 states; 2 ferry crossings; great lake views and riding; especially on the 50-mile ride
32, 42, or 50 miles	Moderate	Quiet back roads; St. Albans; dairy farms; lakeside riding
36 or 59 miles	Moderate (36); moderate to difficult (59)	Lunch in Quebec! Easy riding in farming regions; Philipsburg; Frelighsburg
25 or 41 miles	Easy to moderate	Quebec start; Route de Vin winery; Philipsburg; Mystic; chocolatier
26 or 32 miles	Easy	Great family ride with magnificent lake views; tiny stone castles; split-rail fences and optional ferry ride to Cumberland Head
10 or 21 miles	Easy	St. Anne Shrine; quiet and child-safe roads; Chazy equatorial reefs; lakeside riding; Black Sun Vineyards

TOUR	REGION	TERRAIN
14. Gordon Landing–Rouses Point	Lake Champlain Islands	Flat to lightly rolling
15. Champlain–Mooers	New York Northern	Flat to lightly rolling
16. Plattsburgh–Dannemora	New York Northern	Moderately to seriously rolling (46); rolling to mountainous (59)
17. South Plattsburgh–Peru	New York Northern	Lightly rolling (19, 25); moderately rolling (46)
18. Keeseville–Jay	New York Central	Lightly rolling (13); moderately to seriously rolling
19. Essex–Whallonsburg	New York Central	Lightly to moderately rolling
20. Westport Loops	New York Central	Lightly rolling (12); moderately rolling with one long climb (23)
21. Moriah–North Hudson	New York Southern	Lightly to moderately rolling
22. Ticonderoga–Ironville	New York Southern	Moderately rolling; one long climb
23. Ticonderoga–Chimney Point	New York Southern	Lightly to moderately rolling
24. Burlington–Lake Placid (Keene for 82)	Multiple-day	Lightly rolling to mountainous
25. Whitehall to Montreal	Multiple-day	Some of everything

DISTANCE	DIFFICULTY	HIGHLIGHTS
59 or 69 miles	Moderate	Loop around NW corner of the lake with optional extension into Quebec; lake views and lakeside riding; 2-day trip possible
34, 42, or 50 miles	Easy	Very quiet, well-paved roads; placid countryside; Miner Museum (34); lakeside riding; Rouses Point (optional)
46 or 59 miles	Moderate to difficult (46); challenging (59)	Magical stone walls (46); great descent back to Plattsburgh; outdoor sculpture at SUNY–Plattsburgh
19, 25, or 46 miles	Easy (19, 25); moderate (46)	Apple orchards (19 and 25); deep Adirondack woods; Salmon River Valley (46)
13, 27, 35 or 43 miles	Easy (13); moderate to difficult based on mileage	Excellent Adirondack views from rolling roads; follow the Ausable River back to the start
25 or 35 miles	Moderate	Wonderful back roads with mountain views; glorious lake views and shoreline riding
12 or 23 miles	Easy (12); moderate (23)	Westport; lake and Green Mountain views; quiet farm road; Wadhams (23)
31 miles	Moderate	Quiet and twisting backcountry roads along streams; Adirondack woodlands; cooling "ice mine"
23 miles	Moderate	Upland lakeshore riding; Ironville; Penfield Museum; delightful descents; fish hatchery
43 or 51 miles	Moderate	Cable ferry; rolling farmland; Middlebury College Museum of Art; lake views; historic forts
109 miles (2 days); 82 miles (1 day)	Difficult	Glorious Adirondack riding and views; long descents on return trip; 2 ferry crossings
500 or less	Some of everything	Complete circumnavigation of lake; extension to Montreal

INTRODUCTION The Lake Champlain region is the premier cycling destination in New England, with outstanding scenery, lightly traveled roads, attractive and historic towns and villages, and a wide range of lodging and dining options. This book offers rides over the entire region, from the southern tip of the lake in Whitehall, New York, to its northernmost bay in Quebec, west to Lake Placid and extending east to the charming college town of Middlebury. We have tried to create a book which suits the needs of all cyclists, whether you're a casual rider looking for easy rides in the 10–30-mile range, a hardcore "roadie" seeking challenging day rides of up to 80 miles, or a touring cyclist interested in "credit card" weekend tours.

I have been cycling and leading group tours in this region for some two decades. Although there are many places where I find a single cycling exploration will satisfy me, I keep returning to Lake Champlain year after year with continued enjoyment and satisfaction. I ascribe much of this to a certain serene and sublime quality generated by the lake itself, but at other times it is the high drama of clouds and waves on the lake which stirs me. However, as a cyclist, it may not be the clouds themselves that stir me, but the threat of impending rain or lightning! When you add the beauty and challenge of the Adirondacks to the myriad vistas provided by the lake, the result is a region that provides an almost limitless array of scenic and satisfying rides.

HISTORY The Champlain Basin and its surrounding mountains were created by monumental forces over the past 500 million years. As proof of this, a coral reef from the Equator lies on Isle La Motte (see tour 13). The Champlain Sea was once a part of the Atlantic Ocean, until shifting landmasses left it as a freshwater lake, the sixth largest in the

country. Man first appeared some 8,000 years ago, as the Ice Age glaciers retreated to Canada. When Europeans first arrived, the Algonquins controlled much of the eastern shore of the lake and what is now
Canada, while the five tribes of the Iroquois nation—notably the
Mohawks in the Adirondacks—held the western shore and southern
lands. The western Abenaki tribe lived in a large permanent village
near the mouth of the Missisquoi River until about 1758, and still
maintains a tribal council office in the town of Swanton. Early settlement by whites was difficult as the lake was the main military route in
the lengthy battle between England and France for domination of the
continent. The cessation of the Revolutionary War was a major impetus
for settlement and development, with newfound stability in the region
and land grants to former soldiers. Some of the local history starting
around this time is contained in the descriptions of towns within the
tours.

Lake Champlain is 120 miles long, 20 miles at its widest, and up to
400 feet deep; it covers 435 square miles and drains north through the
Richelieu River to the St. Lawrence River. Comparing this to Lake
Ontario—the smallest of the Great Lakes at 7,340 square miles—gives
you some understanding of the reaction in some parts when Lake
Champlain was designated the country's "Sixth Great Lake" on March
5, 1998. With his signature on Senate Bill 927, President Bill Clinton
included Lake Champlain in legislation reauthorizing the Sea Grant
Program, which provides grants to study environmental issues con-
cerning the Great Lakes. This inclusion, engineered by Senator Patrick
Leahy of Vermont, gives colleges in Vermont greater eligibility when
applying for federal grants to study the Great Lakes' ecological and
historical impacts. On March 24 Senator Leahy joined other senators
in removing Lake Champlain as an official Great Lake, while still
including it for grant purposes, stating: "We have agreed to call Lake
Champlain a cousin instead of a little brother to those larger lakes in
the Midwest."

ABOUT THE TOURS The tours have been selected to provide rides in a
variety of regions around the lake as well as varying lengths and
degrees of challenge to meet the needs of all cyclists. At the extreme
ends of the spectrum is tour 13, which offers a flat and easy 10-mile
ride around historic Isle La Motte, to the 1-day option of tour 24, a

challenging 82-mile Adirondack sampler covering two states while taking two ferries.

We have tried to use roads that are scenic, well paved and lightly traveled, but it is not always possible to find roads that meet all these criteria in each area. Some tours include sections of riding with moderate traffic, but in all cases we consider those roads safe for cycling and the traffic a minor trade-off for an otherwise fine tour route. You will notice that a number of the rides share common sections of road in their routes. In situations where there is a particular road that is significantly more bike-friendly than others in the area, I have routed multiple tours over that segment rather than use less attractive or safe roads.

I have tried to provide multiple distances for the tours whenever possible. Nineteen of the 23 day-rides offer multiple choices; in some cases I've given 3 or 4 ride lengths, and often other options or variations. There are many benefits to this; among them are:

If a group of riders with varying mileage/difficulty preferences wants to ride together, they can do so for part of the tour, perhaps meeting later at a specified point after doing different loops in the middle of the ride.

A negative change in the weather may unexpectedly cause you to desire a shorter ride.

A mechanical problem or some minor injury or other medical situation may call for a quicker return to the start than planned.

A choice of distances during the ride allows a rider to select the route based on how you feel at each split point, as you may start riding without being certain how energetic you'll feel that day.

If you do the same tour multiple times, the options allow you to change the route you ride for variety.

Assigning the Terrain and Difficulty rating for each tour was somewhat daunting. While the former is generally straightforward, the latter seems highly subjective, despite other author's attempts to codify things based on gradient, length, and frequency of climbs. I only call a ride "flat" when it is almost virtually flat the entire distance or close to it. However, most rides will have some flat sections, even when I describe it as seriously "rolling" or mountainous. "Rolling" means that most of the ride is either going up or down; the qualifiers lightly, moderately, and seriously connote the general steepness and duration of the uphill segments. The "easy," " moderate," "difficult," and "challenging" ratings are my appraisal of the ride's overall difficulty. I have no qualms in calling a 50-mile ride "easy" if the terrain is flat and lightly rolling. On the other hand, steep climbing can make a 20-mile ride difficult. I have tried to be consistent and hope that after a ride or two you will have an understanding of my terms and how they relate to your tastes and abilities as a cyclist.

FOUR EASY RULES FOR STAYING ON THE ROUTE

- Always know what the next turn is and anticipate it. Be aware of the next action you need to take and about when that will occur, either time- or mileage-wise. It's actually best to have read the next two cues, because sometimes a turn will closely follow another.

- Always ride straight at any intersection unless otherwise directed. If there is no choice that goes exactly straight, select the road this is the straightest, while also applying the next rule.

- Always stay on the major road at any fork, or with the signed (numbered or named) road that you've been on, unless otherwise directed.

- Never be tempted to ride on a dirt road unless the cue specifically mentions it. Outside of tour 12 and two other tours with mile-long dirt segments, there are no situations where the tours in this book go off the pavement.

Be aware that things can change. Road signs can be knocked down by snowplows and new ones erected with a different name than shown on maps. If uncertain, try finding someone to ask, but if a road goes in the correct direction at the mileage given in the cues, it is almost certainly the road you want even if the sign (or lack thereof) does not match what is in the book.

SAFETY AND RIDING TIPS The single most important step to take in improving safety is to wear a helmet when you ride. It will not help prevent accidents, but it will greatly diminish your risk of serious head injury if you do have an accident.

Not far behind wearing a helmet in importance is using a mirror, which I consider one of the best ways to reduce the risk of an accident. Some folks like the helmet-mounted mirrors, but I much prefer those mounted on the bike. Instead of just hearing the advance of a vehicle from the rear, the mirror will show the type of vehicle and how close it is to you. I also use the mirror to be particularly cautious when a truck is approaching from one direction and another vehicle may be passing at the same time the truck will pass me. Normally I would expect the vehicle behind me to brake and wait until it is safe to pass, but if that doesn't seem to be happening I will get as far over to the right as possible. Mirrors are also helpful for keeping track of the other members of your group.

Check your bike thoroughly before you start riding, especially if it's your first ride of the season or in a long time. Make sure that your tires are in good condition (no signs of cuts or cracking) and properly inflated, the wheels tightly attached, brakes and shifters are working and all bolts and nuts are tight. If you haven't ridden your bike for at least a year you might want to have your local shop check it over for you. However, I strongly encourage you to learn how to repair your own flat tires (some bike shops hold classes) and to carry the necessary equipment to do so—a working pump that fits your valves, a spare tube or two, patch kit, and tire levers.

Always ride with traffic and follow all traffic laws and road signs. Signal your turns to fellow riders and drivers. John Forester, the dean of bicycle safety in America and creator of the Effective Cyclist program, writes: "Cyclists fare best when they act and are treated as drivers of vehicles." This means that you should follow vehicular laws but at the same time expect the same rights and courtesy as any other vehicle.

When making a turn, position yourself in the lane based on your destination direction. If turning left, move to the left side of the lane AFTER checking that it is clear behind you and signaling the turn.

Watch for cars pulling out of side streets, driveways, parking lots, and roadside businesses. Also be conscious of parked cars along the road in villages and ride far enough out that a suddenly opened door won't catch you.

Be attentive to the road surface and keep both hands on the handlebars. Actively look for potholes, broken glass, sandy patches near the edge of the road, and other hazards that could cause you a problem. If you see a hazard up ahead, and there are other riders following you, call out "Glass!" or "Hole!" and also point to the problem area so they know where it is and can avoid it. If you are uncomfortable descending quickly by all means apply the brakes, but make sure you use equal pressure on each brake lever and pump them on and off instead of maintaining continuous tight pressure, which can cause rims to overheat and brakes to fail on long and/or steep downhills.

When crossing railroad tracks, do so at a right angle or as close to it as possible. If this is difficult due to traffic in a given situation, get off your bike and walk across. Rails at an extreme diagonal to the road can easily catch your front wheel if crossed at a shallow angle. (I have emphasized this with a caution note in the text's cues when I am aware of this situation on the tours.) Also be extra cautious when the tracks are wet since they're very slippery then. The same holds true for bridges with a grated metal surface, and many riders will always walk across such bridges, as the surface can be slippery for bike tires even when dry.

Dogs are more of a nuisance than a danger, but the problem is that you never know in advance. The technique that I find works best is to point a finger directly at the dog and in your firmest voice yell "No" as loudly as you possibly can. My feeling is that other traditional approaches, such as waving a pump or spraying water from your bottle, take too much time and create a risk of you losing control of your bike. Another recommended technique is to get off your bike and keep it between the dog and yourself.

Stay to the right and ride single file whenever the road or traffic warrants it. Some would say to do this always, but many roads used for these tours are so lightly traveled that with a good sight line you can ride next to someone as long as both of you pay attention for approaching traffic, blind turns and crests, or other situations where you need to be in single file.

WHAT TO BRING

- **A handlebar bar, preferably with a transparent map-pocket on top.** I keep my 35mm SLR camera on a foam pad cushion in the main compartment and wallet, keys, sunglasses, and so forth are kept in the front compartment. The best style here is when no bungee-type straps are required, which will provide quick release and reattachment. For those who don't like to mount a "bar bag" on their bike, I suggest a separate map case and recommend those made by BarMap in a number of sizes. Also, there's always the low-tech technique of using a binder clip to attach the cues to a cable on the bike. Rather than mangle this book by trying to keep it open to the right page during the ride, I suggest either removing the pages for the tour you want to do or photocopying them. Alternatives to the bar bag include a rack bag if you have a rear rack mounted on your bike or one of the newer style racks that mount off the seat post.

- **A tool kit.** As previously mentioned, it is highly recommended to have the knowledge and equipment/tools to repair your own flat tires. A minimal tool kit would also include a set of Allen wrenches, separate hex wrenches or a 6-inch adjustable wrench, screwdriver, some extra bolts and nuts and electrical tape. Several handy all-in-one tools are made nowadays that have most of these as a single unit.

- **Filled water bottle(s).** Your bike should have at least one water bottle mount if not two and you should make sure the bottle(s) are filled before beginning your ride. Some riders prefer the hydration systems that are worn on your back. You may be able to find a store to get water if you forget or need a refill, or if desperate you can always approach a house on the route, but it's always best to have your bottles filled in advance.

- **Food or snacks.** Depending on the length of your tour, you may or may not want a full meal while on the ride. Some riders don't like to stop for extended periods after they're warmed up, but I like to have a relaxed midday meal on a long ride. However, always carry some emergency rations in case you find yourself needing quick energy far from the nearest town or store. Energy and candy bars or fruit work well for this, but each rider usually has their own preferences here.

- **A bike computer or cyclometer**. The cues are based on the mileage from the start at the turn, or other notation, in the book. It is possible to navigate strictly from the map if you're a spatially oriented person, but most folks are happier matching up the cues to the mileage on their computer. Many of these rides are in areas where it's all too easy to become enamored with the bucolic scenery and forget about following the cues. That's fine as long as you don't mind a somewhat longer ride than you anticipated.

- **A lock.** Again, for the most part, the tours in this book are in rural areas—not necessarily known as bicycle-theft territory—yet a stolen bike will surely ruin your day, weekend, or vacation. My own view is that you'll be better off with a strong cable lock instead of a U-type lock in this region. Generally speaking you won't be leaving your bike for an extended period and the lock acts more as assurance that the bike won't walk away while you're having lunch vs. absolute security against a determined thief. One benefit of the cable lock is that you can loop it through both of your wheels and the stationary object to which you're locking it. You can also lock the bike to a tree, though the U-lock is out if its element for this. If you're leaving the bike while in an urban area, you might also consider removing anything that a thief or vandal could easily take, such as a pump or pannier. I keep all my valuables in my handlebar bag and generally take that with me when leaving the bike, even if I am not locking it.

- **Clothing.** Bike gloves are recommended primarily to give the nerves in your hands some padding (the gel models are especially good for this), but also as a point of contact between your hand and the road if you should ever dismount in an accident. I find it uncomfortable to ride more than a few miles without padded bike shorts, but then I have a woman friend who rides a "century" (100 miles) in the thinnest of running shorts. No doubt you'll find out what your comfort needs are after your first few rides. In the summer you will rarely need more than a rain jacket besides the clothes you're riding in, but in spring and fall bring a long-sleeve polypro (or similar wicking material) top and tights, as well as polypro liner gloves and some form of head cover. A cotton T-shirt is fine as long as the weather is dry and warm, but you definitely don't want wet cotton next to your skin if the weather is cool. Try to dress in multiple light layers, which gives you much more flexibility than something bulky such as a fleece jacket.
- **A bicycle light.** If you think there's any chance that you'll be riding in the dusk or dark, carry a strong headlight for the front and a flasher for the rear. There are no streetlights on the country roads that these tours use, so you'll literally be caught in the dark if you don't have a light.

HOW TO USE THIS BOOK A lot will depend on where you're coming from, not to mention how much time you have available and the length of ride you prefer. We've tried hard to provide tours for all tastes in the many regions around the lake, so that you can find a tour of the length and difficulty you want without much travel. The Tours at a Glance can be very helpful in selecting a tour that's right for you. I recommend reading the entire tour description and cues before riding it as well as the regional introduction, which will provide other useful information.

If you live in the region you can do all the rides that interest you over a period of time, perhaps doing some of them that are farther away as part of a weekend trip. Those traveling a longer distance to get to the region will want to plan ahead to make the best use of their time while here. If you don't mind carrying your own gear, you may want to try the Adirondack Weekender overnight tour or even the Grand Tour circumnavigating the lake. Other multiple-day trips are possible by combining some of the routes and using the ferries crossing Lake Champlain in four locations and the one bridge; see the multiple-day tour section of the book for suggestions of possible routes.

I suggest photocopying the cues for the ride(s) that you plan to do. This saves you from having to either mangle the book with repeated folds to use it during the ride, or tearing out the pages. Another benefit is that you'll feel less guilty making notes on the copied sheets or using a highlighter to emphasize sections of interest. Also, if doing a tour that has multiple distance options, you can customize the cue mileages for the loop that you intend to do.

A note on the cues: I use the plus symbol (+) to indicate a turn that is less than 1/10 mile after the previous cue.

MAPS I highly recommend the excellent Lake Champlain Region map published by Northern Cartographic and encourage riders to carry it while biking. You won't need it for the actual tour route, but it does provide some perspective on distant sights, especially when riding next to the lake. This map will also assist you with driving in the region, particularly in getting to the start of the tours. This same company also publishes large-scale road maps of Addison County and Chittenden County, the city of Burlington, and northwestern Vermont, which cover all the rides in Vermont. Jimapco and others publish maps of Clinton and Essex Counties in New York State; tours 1 and 2 are in Washington County. The Lake Champlain map covers almost all the routes in Quebec, with the exception of the final 7 miles in tour 11.

NOTES ON BORDERS AND FOR RIDERS COMING FROM CANADA If doing any of the tours that cross the U.S. and Canada border (10, 11 or 14), it is essential that you carry at least one photo ID with you. Although cyclists are generally questioned less than people in cars, you'll probably be asked to show your ID at the border Customs station. The crossings that these tours use generally have short lines, but this can depend on the day and season.

Avoid the US 87 (Northway)/Canada 15 crossing in Champlain, as this gets the majority of the through traffic between the United States and Montreal, and it can be particularly slow coming into the States. If driving south on 15, I recommend taking the last exit in Canada, which you'll probably anticipate due to the long line of cars ahead. This exit is probably signed for Montee Glass and/or Montee Guay. Turn east and drive a couple of miles to Quebec 221 and turn right, which will become Clinton 276 in the United States. If you miss this, turn right on Quebec 223 at a T-intersection, which will bring you into Rouses Point. In general, the smaller border crossings will be much faster than the large ones and those at Alburg and Morses Line are also good places to cross.

OTHER RESOURCES Lake Champlain Bikeways (LCB) is a public/private partnership group whose goal is to develop and promote economic growth through bicycle tourism in the greater Lake Champlain region. They've designated a principal route around the lake that includes dirt roads (sometimes very rough) and an all-paved alternate route where the principal route does wander off the pavement. The Lake Champlain region map highlights the routes used by Lake Champlain Bikeways as well as the "Theme Loops" that have been created by local areas around the lake. Cues for these routes are on the regional map and also available on the LCB site: (http://www.champlainbikeways .org/ or 802-652-BIKE); they also have guides for the various Theme Loops available for free.

WHITEHALL AND THE SOUTH AREA TOURS

Whitehall waterfront and Skene Manor

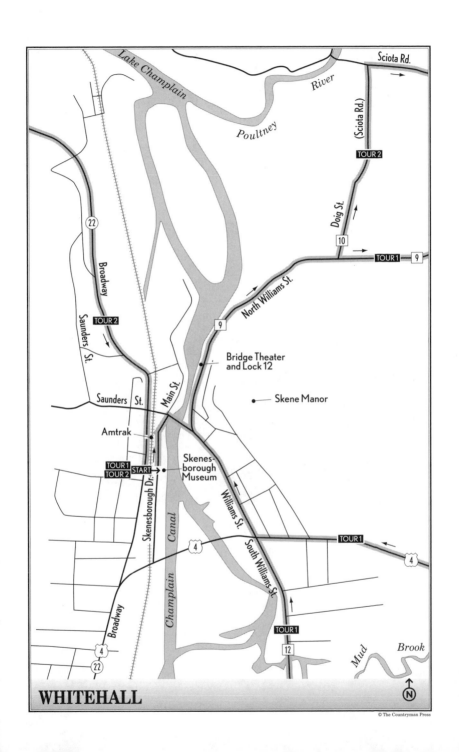

WHITEHALL

WHEN I WAS DEVELOPING my weeklong TALCAM tour (Tour Around Lake Champlain, Adirondacks, and Montreal), I selected Whitehall as the starting point for a number of reasons. It is the geographical southern end of the lake; the Lake Champlain Bikeways (LCB) route starts from here; and it is the closest point on the route to the urban centers where I expected most of the riders to come from. All of the above points also have some relevance for this book and the last is particularly true for riders coming from the Albany area or anywhere near the Northway, all the way down to New York City and beyond. One other benefit is that Amtrak's "Adirondack" stops here once a day in each direction and the dedicated baggage car has "roll-on" bike service, meaning that you don't need to box your bike, although a reservation is required. Although Whitehall does have limited lodging and dining options, I recommend that folks coming from any distance for a ride spend the previous night in either Rutland or the Glen Falls areas, where there is a far greater range of tourist facilities. Whitehall is about a half-hour drive from either location.

Founded in 1759 as the town of Skenesborough by British army captain Philip Skene, Whitehall was the first permanent settlement on Lake Champlain. In May 1775, the town was captured by Revolutionary forces, and Benedict Arnold armed Captain Skene's schooner and used it to capture a British ship later in the same month. The following year Congress authorized the construction of a fleet of ships, which in October engaged the superior British fleet in an important delaying action near Valcour Island, thereby saving the American forces camped at Saratoga. Whitehall is one of several locations with a claim to the title of "Birthplace of the U.S. Navy."

Although Whitehall's glory years are behind it, the village is making an effort at invigorating its downtown area. In 2001 it opened the Skenesborough Harbor Park and also boasts the unique Bridge Theater, which was built inside an unused truss bridge over the Champlain Canal's Lock 12 that connects the canal to the lake. While in town you may want to visit the Skene Manor, which is impossible to miss with its hillside perch overlooking the entire downtown area. The Skenesborough Museum is recommended for a background on village and area history. It includes a 16-foot-long diorama of the 1776 shipyard, showing the fledgling American fleet under construction.

Tourism Info

The Whitehall Chamber of Commerce, 259 Broadway, Whitehall, NY 12887 (http://www.whitehallchamber.com/)

Bike Shops

There are none in Whitehall, so make certain that your bike is in good condition before starting any of the rides in this region. The nearest shops are:

Green Mountain Cyclery, 133 Strongs Avenue, Rutland (802-775-0869)

Sports Peddler, 158 N Main Street # 3, Rutland (802-775-0101)

Inside Edge Ski & Bike Shop, 643 Upper Glen Street, Queensbury (518-793-5676)

1

Whitehall–Fair Haven

*Back roads and rolling hills
across two states*

- **DISTANCE:** 23 or 32 miles.
- **TERRAIN/DIFFICULTY:** Moderately to more seriously rolling; moderately difficult.
- **START:** Skenesborough Museum, located on Skenesborough Drive between US 4 and Saunders Street in downtown Whitehall.
- **GETTING THERE/PARKING:** From New York State take I-87 to Exit 20 and then NY 149 east to US 4 north to Whitehall; from Vermont take US 4 west to Rutland and Whitehall. There is some parking at the museum itself and additional parking along Skenesborough Drive.

These loops both pass through Fair Haven, Vermont, a picturesque village with some of the best examples of Victorian architecture in the state. It was chartered in 1779 by Matthew Lyon, an Irish-born entrepreneur who built sawmills and paper mills, as well as being owner of the town's first store, inn, and newspaper. Fair Haven today is a major center in the slate industry, and you may wish to visit the Slate Valley Museum in nearby Granville, NY, although it's somewhat off the cycling route.

The route out of Whitehall is as rolling as rolling can get. None of the climbs are particularly steep or long, but it does seem as if there's an endless supply of them. Things flatten out approaching Fair Haven where both loops head south on VT 22A, which may have some traffic but is level and a decent cycling road with a rideable shoulder. The short ride has 5 hilly miles on Washington County 18 back to Whitehall, while the longer loop continues on VT 22A for 5 miles farther and then takes local back roads and the lovely Washington County 12 back

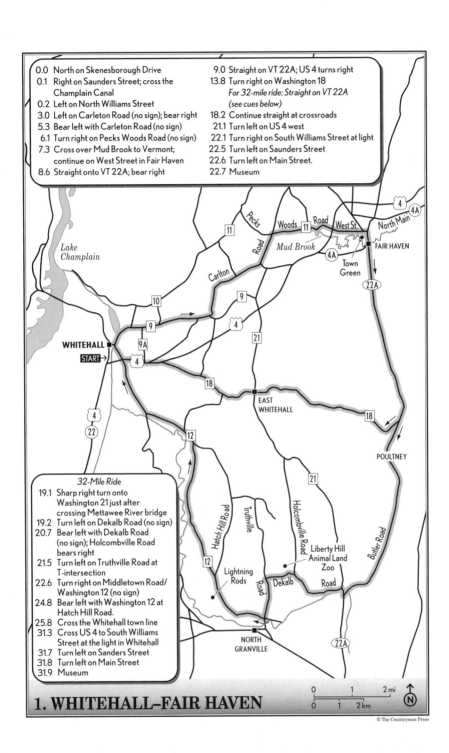

0.0   North on Skenesborough Drive
0.1   Right on Saunders Street; cross the
      Champlain Canal
0.2   Left on North Williams Street
3.0   Left on Carleton Road (no sign); bear right
5.3   Bear left with Carleton Road (no sign)
6.1   Turn right on Pecks Woods Road (no sign)
7.3   Cross over Mud Brook to Vermont;
      continue on West Street in Fair Haven
8.6   Straight onto VT 22A; bear right

9.0   Straight on VT 22A; US 4 turns right
13.8 Turn right on Washington 18
      *For 32-mile ride: Straight on VT 22A
      (see cues below)*
18.2 Continue straight at crossroads
21.1 Turn left on US 4 west
22.1 Turn right on South Williams Street at light
22.5 Turn left on Saunders Street
22.6 Turn left on Main Street.
22.7 Museum

32-Mile Ride

19.1 Sharp right turn onto
      Washington 21 just after
      crossing Mettawee River bridge
19.2 Turn left on Dekalb Road (no sign)
20.7 Bear left with Dekalb Road
      (no sign); Holcombville Road
      bears right
21.5 Turn left on Truthville Road at
      T-intersection
22.6 Turn right on Middletown Road/
      Washington 12 (no sign)
24.8 Bear left with Washington 12 at
      Hatch Hill Road.
25.8 Cross the Whitehall town line
31.3 Cross US 4 to South Williams
      Street at the light in Whitehall
31.7 Turn left on Sanders Street
31.8 Turn left on Main Street
31.9 Museum

Lake
Champlain

WHITEHALL
START→

Pecks
Woods Road
West St.
North Main
Mud Brook
FAIR HAVEN
Town
Green
Carlton
Road

EAST
WHITEHALL

POULTNEY

Hatch Hill Road
Truthville
Holcombville Road
Butler Road
Liberty Hill
Animal Land
Zoo
Lightning
Rods
Dekalb   Road

NORTH
GRANVILLE

0   1   2 mi
0   1   2 km

N

1. WHITEHALL–FAIR HAVEN

© The Countryman Press

to the start. Although relatively short, either loop will give you a good workout as they're largely continuously rolling with the exception of the mileage on 22A.

0.0 North on Skenesborough Drive from the museum entrance.

You can see Skene Manor perched on the hillside across the river.

0.1 Turn Right on Saunders street and cross the Champlain Canal.

Looking to your left you see Lock #12, which connects the canal (and through it the Hudson River) to Lake Champlain.

0.2 Turn left on North Williams Street.

Note the heavily decorated old buildings on the left and then the Bridge Theater built inside the old truss bridge over Lock #12. This road seems to be under permanent construction and may be bumpy here, but will soon smooth out.

0.9 Continue straight at the sign for Washington 9.

3.0 Bear left on Carleton Road (no sign) where the main road bears right.

5.3 Bear left with Carleton Road (no sign).

6.1 Turn right on Pecks Woods Road (no sign) at the four-way intersection.

7.3 Cross Mud Brook and enter Vermont—you're now on West Street entering Fair Haven.

8.6 Continue straight ahead onto VT 22A south in Fair Haven—moderate traffic here.

Fair Haven is the only town that either loop passes through, so if you need any food or other supplies this is the time to get them. There is also an expansive town green which makes a good location for a break, or to eat your lunch if you're ready for it.

8.6+ Bear right with VT 22A south as it curves around the green.

You may wish to do an extra loop around the green to view the magnificent houses fronting on it, or even spend a while exploring the quiet side streets of Fair Haven.

9.0 Continue straight on VT 22A where US 4A goes right.

13.7 Sam's Dog House, a summer only snack stand, is on the left.

13.8 Turn right on Washington 18—be ready for some climbing over the next 5 miles.

For 32-mile ride: *Ride straight on VT 22A and continue with the cues below.*

18.2 Continue straight at the crossroads—it will be mostly downhill from here.

21.1 Turn left on US 4 west at a T-intersection; this road is busy but there's a good shoulder.

22.1 Turn right on South Williams Street at the light.

22.5 Turn left on Saunders street and cross the Champlain Canal—this should look familiar!

22.6 Turn left on Main Street.

22.7 Skenesborough Museum—end of the tour.

32-MILE RIDE

19.1 Make a sharp right turn onto Washington 21 just after crossing the bridge over the Mettawee River.

19.2 Turn left on Dekalb Road (no sign).

20.7 Bear left with Dekalb Road (no sign) where Holcombville Road bears right.

20.9 Liberty Hill Animal Land Zoo is on the right up a dirt road.
Posted hours are Monday–Saturday 10–6 and Sunday 1–6; admission fee.

21.5 Turn left on Truthville Road at the T-intersection (or suffer the consequences!).

22.6 Turn right on Middletown Road/Washington 12 (no sign).
This is an exceptional cycling road, with (mostly) gently rolling hills, smooth pavement, little traffic and wonderful scenery.

24.2 There is a truly impressive display of lightning rods at the farmstead on the left.
I counted 34 rods in total, often with 3 to 5 on a single roof. I don't know if this was based

An open road and cloudy skies on NY 22A

on an engineering nature, a previous bad experience, or just paranoia.

24.8 Bear left with Washington 12 at Hatch Hill Road.

25.8 As you cross the Whitehall town line the nature of the road changes dramatically, starting with a very fast downhill. The next 4 miles provide exhilarating riding.

29.8 Just at the right turn in the road is a pair of beautiful wooden cupolas, probably off an old barn.

31.3 Cross US 4 to South Williams Street at the light in Whitehall.

31.7 Turn left on Sanders Street.

31.8 Turn left on Main Street.

31.9 Skenesborough Museum —end of the tour.

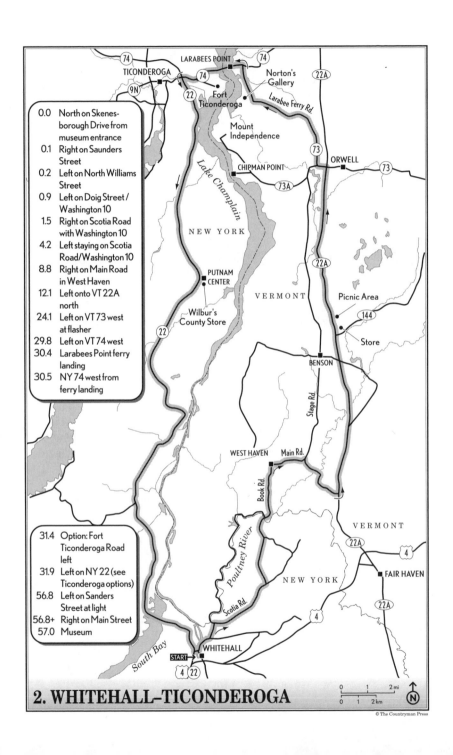

0.0	North on Skenes-borough Drive from museum entrance
0.1	Right on Saunders Street
0.2	Left on North Williams Street
0.9	Left on Doig Street / Washington 10
1.5	Right on Scotia Road with Washington 10
4.2	Left staying on Scotia Road/Washington 10
8.8	Right on Main Road in West Haven
12.1	Left onto VT 22A north
24.1	Left on VT 73 west at flasher
29.8	Left on VT 74 west
30.4	Larabees Point ferry landing
30.5	NY 74 west from ferry landing

31.4	Option: Fort Ticonderoga Road left
31.9	Left on NY 22 (see Ticonderoga options)
56.8	Left on Sanders Street at light
56.8+	Right on Main Street
57.0	Museum

TICONDEROGA

LARABEES POINT

Norton's Gallery

Fort Ticonderoga

Larabee Ferry Rd.

Mount Independence

CHIPMAN POINT

ORWELL

Lake Champlain

NEW YORK

PUTNAM CENTER

VERMONT

Picnic Area

Wilbur's County Store

Store

BENSON

Stage Rd.

WEST HAVEN

Main Rd.

Book Rd.

Poultney River

VERMONT

FAIR HAVEN

NEW YORK

Scotia Rd.

South Bay

WHITEHALL

START

2. WHITEHALL-TICONDEROGA

| 0 | 1 | 2 mi |
| 0 | 1 | 2 km |

Whitehall–Ticonderoga

Hills, history, and a cable ferry

- **DISTANCE:** 57 miles.

- **TERRAIN/DIFFICULTY:** Gently rolling northbound with a seriously rolling return; moderately difficult.

- **START:** Skenesborough Museum, located on Skenesborough Drive between US 4 and Saunders Street in downtown Whitehall.

- **GETTING THERE/PARKING:** From New York State take I-87 to Exit 20 and then NY 149 east to US 4 north to Whitehall; from Vermont take US 4 west to Rutland and Whitehall. There is some parking at the museum itself and additional parking along Skenesborough Drive.

Leaving Whitehall you soon encounter rolling hills, but are well compensated as you experience some beautiful, bucolic scenery. After crossing the Poultney River into Vermont you will pass through the small village of West Haven, barely more than a crossroad. We take VT 22A for 12 miles and this can have moderate traffic, but there is usually a rideable shoulder. Turn off VT 22A and soon you'll have your first views of Lake Champlain with the southern Adirondacks in the distance as you head for the Ticonderoga Ferry. This is one of the oldest continuously running ferries in the country and uses cables to guide the boat across one of the narrowest sections of the lake.

Once across you have a very short ride to Fort Ticonderoga. Even if you don't wish to pay the admission to see the entire restored fort and costumed performers (reenactors?), I strongly recommend the mile-long ride down to it through a tree-lined avenue. There are plentiful markers describing the grounds and the many military actions that took place here. At the end of the road you'll find a restaurant, a well-

Cyclists climbing from the lake near Larabees Point

stocked book and gift shop, and views of the fort and surrounding lake. Another optional side trip while in the Ticonderoga vicinity is a climb up Mount Defiance for a truly splendid view of the lake, the fort and the extensive farmland across the lake in Vermont. The town also provides the only opportunity on this loop for a sit-down meal besides the fort.

After you're done exploring you have a hilly return to Whitehall, but on an excellent road with lane-wide, well-paved shoulders and wonderful open views of the surrounding countryside. For riders who prefer a slower pace, this ride can also be done in two days with an overnight in Ticonderoga, or combined with tour 23 for an extended 2–3-day tour.

0.0 Ride north on Skenesborough Drive from the museum entrance.

You can see Skene Manor perched on the hillside across the river.

0.1 Turn right on Saunders Street and cross the Champlain Canal.

Looking to your left you see Lock #12 which connects the canal (and through it the Hudson River) to Lake Champlain.

0.2 Leaving the bridge turn left on North Williams Street.

Note the heavily decorated old buildings on the left and the Bridge Theater on the truss bridge over the lock. The road is very bumpy here, but will soon smooth out.

0.9 Turn left on Doig Street signed for Washington 10.

1.5 Turn right on Scotia Road with Washington 10—the next several miles are seriously rolling, but in a lovely landscape.

4.2 Turn left staying on Scotia Road/Washington 10.

6.7 A downhill leads to the crossing of Poultney River into Vermont, followed by a climb on Book Road.

8.8 Turn right on Main Road (signed for 22A) in West Haven after passing the sweet little church.

10.1 After crossing the Hubbardton River bridge at the bottom of this downhill, you have a final stiff climb before gaining flatter terrain.

12.1 Turn left onto VT 22A north at the T-intersection—the shoulder width varies but is almost always rideable.

17.9 At the junction with VT 144 there is a country store on the right with a port-a-potty out front—this is your best opportunity for supplies before Ticonderoga.

18.6 There is a pleasant state picnic area on the right that makes a good place to take an early lunch or just a break from riding, but there are no facilities.

24.1 Turn left on VT 73 west at the flasher—there is a small store at the turn.
If you're willing to make a side trip, the pretty village of Orwell is .3 to the right on VT 73 east and claims to have the smallest bank building in the country. Orwell also has a general store and a country diner.

24.4 Turn right with VT 73 west.
Going straight here on Chipman Point Road/VT 73A will bring you to Mount Independence (named by the troops in honor of the new Declaration of Independence), a prominence rising across the lake from Fort Ticonderoga. Here American soldiers occupied fortifications from June 1776 until July the following year, when the site was abandoned in the face of a superior British advance. There is a visitors center and museum at the site, but getting there will require a long ride on a dead-end road.

28.4 As you turn right where the road approaches the lake, looking across you can clearly see the red roofs of Fort Ticonderoga.

28.5 On the left is Norton's Gallery, which specializes in playful sculpted animals and figures. If you turn around after passing the gallery you will see a depiction of Grant Wood's *American Gothic* painted on the end wall.

29.8 Turn left on VT 74 west for the Ticonderoga ferry.

30.1 On the right there is a mural painted on the side of the barn and to the left there are spools of cable for the ferry, which needs replacing every four years.

30.4 Larabees Point ferry landing. If the ferry is not there when you arrive, it will either be in transit or loading on the NY shore.

30.5 Ride on NY 74 west from the Ticonderoga ferry landing.

The railroad track you will soon cross carries the daily Amtrak "Adirondack" between Washington and Montreal; this train features a dedicated baggage car that provides roll-on (no requirement to pack in a box) bike service; however, you must make advance reservations.

31.4 Option 1: Fort Ticonderoga Road turns sharply left here through the entrance gate.

It is 1 mile to the fort and well worth the trip, but do note that it is a downhill run so you'll be climbing on the way back. The fort is open daily 9–5 PM (6 PM in July and August) from early May to late October; admission fee.

31.9 Turn left on NY 22 south and get ready for some climbing, as you have rolling hills most of the way to Whitehall.

Note: *If taking either of the below options, return to this intersection to continue the tour.*

Option 2: Take Montcalm Street (straight across from NY 74) and follow the cues in the Ticonderoga regional intro to climb Mount Defiance.

Option 3: Take Montcalm Street if you want to visit the town of Ticonderoga for food or supplies.

Shortly you'll see a large grassy expanse on the right, which is Centennial Park. You'll also notice the falls of the La Chute River, which was the attraction for the large paper mill which was previously located in this area. After it relocated up-lake, all the old structures were torn down and replaced with today's park and recreational path meandering through it. The exception to this is the former main office building, which now houses the Ticonderoga Heritage Museum; see the regional intro for details.

40.0 Wilbur's Country Store is on the left, which is your only opportunity for food or supplies between Ti and Whitehall.

56.8 Turn left on Sanders Street at the light in Whitehall.

56.8+ Quick turn right on Main Street.

57.0 Skenesborough Museum—end of the tour.

MIDDLEBURY AND THE VERMONT SOUTHERN TOURS

Magnificent Congregational Church steeple in Middlebury

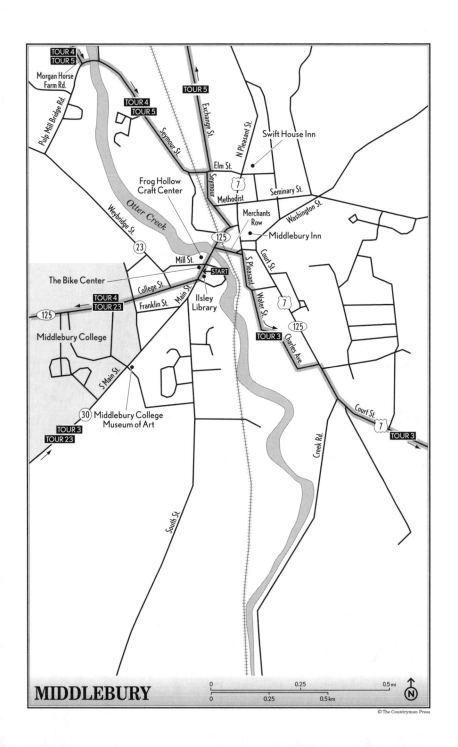

TOUR 4
TOUR 5

Morgan Horse
Farm Rd.

Pulp Mill Bridge Rd.

TOUR 4
TOUR 5

Seymour St.

Exchange St.

TOUR 5

N Pleasant St.

Swift House Inn

Elm St.

Weybridge St.

Otter Creek

Seymour

7

Methodist

Seminary St.

Washington St.

Frog Hollow
Craft Center

23

125

Merchants
Row

Middlebury Inn

Mill St.

START

Court St.

The Bike Center

College St.

S Pleasant

7

125

TOUR 4
TOUR 23

Franklin St.

Main St.

Ilsley
Library

Water St.

TOUR 3

125

Middlebury College

S Main St.

Charles Ave.

30

Middlebury College
Museum of Art

Court St.

7

TOUR 3
TOUR 23

Creek Rd.

TOUR 3

South St.

MIDDLEBURY

0   0.25   0.5 mi

0   0.25   0.5 km

N

© The Countryman Press

MIDDLEBURY IS AT THE CENTER of Addison County and was granted a charter by the governor of New Hampshire (which used to control Vermont) in the name of King George III in 1761, after a successful campaign by the British army to drive the French forces and settlers out of the region. The first Anglo settlers in Middlebury arrived in 1766 and worked the marble quarries and built mills, shops, homes, and churches in the area around Otter Creek Falls.

Middlebury can lay claim to a number of firsts, including well-known educator Emma Hart Willard establishing the first American college for women in Middlebury in 1814. The town was the home of the first Morgan horse (the Morgan Horse Farm is a short ride out of town), and the birthplace of inventor John Deere, who created "the plow that broke the plains."

No discussion of the town is complete without mention of highly regarded Middlebury College, which recently celebrated its bicentennial. The campus of largely traditional architecture has seen some handsome contemporary buildings added in recent years, and provides a rewarding walking or biking exploration. I particularly recommend the excellent art museum, which is on the route of tours 3 and 23.

I suggest allowing time to explore this charming town on foot, whether you're doing a day ride or spending the night there. One strong recommendation is the Frog Hollow Vermont State Craft Center, after which you can continue down the hill (passing Ben & Jerry's, an ever-popular cyclist destination) to the pedestrian bridge, which crosses the river and provides an excellent view of the falls of Otter Creek. It's interesting that it's called a creek, since in fact it's the longest river in the state, although certainly not the most dramatic. On the far side of this bridge are the sprawling 19th-century structures of the Marble Works, where you can still find evidence of the days when these buildings were used to cut and finish the marble brought up from local quarries.

The Middlebury Inn is the major lodging option in the downtown area, although the Swift House Inn is nearby. The inn provides a locked outdoor bike storage area; if you're staying in the motel units (recommended for cyclists) there's plenty of space in these modern, tastefully decorated, and comfortable rooms. The inn's lodging fee, while expensive, includes a most excellent buffet breakfast that will amply fuel any cyclist for an active day. Less expensive motel options are within a few miles of town, and Marriott has a new Courtyard Hotel 1 mile from downtown. One good reason to stay in town is the easy walking access to the many excellent local restaurants. Mister Up's has consistently proven the most popular on my group bike tours through town, with its riverside deck and excellent salad bar. There are several other top choices in town including The Storm Café, Fire and Ice (not the chain), and Tully and Marie's.

Tourism Info

Addison County Chamber of Commerce, 2 Court Street, Middlebury (1-800-SEE-VERMONT or www.midvermont.com)

The Middlebury Business Association publishes a helpful map & guide to Middlebury, which can be found in many locations in town.

Bike Shops

Middlebury—The Bike Center, 74 Main Street (802-388-6666)

Middlebury—Skihaus of Vermont, Merchants Row (802-388-6762)

3

Middlebury–Brandon

Lake Dunmore, Otter Creek, and rolling farmland

- **DISTANCE:** 39 or 56 miles.

- **TERRAIN/DIFFICULTY:** Lightly to moderately rolling with a half-mile steep climb; moderate.

- **START:** Ilsley Public Library, Main Street/VT 30/VT 125 in Middlebury, across from The Bike Center.

- **GETTING THERE/PARKING:** Middlebury isn't near an interstate, so your route there will depend on where you're coming from. It does lie on US 7, which is the major north-south road in western Vermont. There is public parking behind the library and also on Bakery Lane, but be sure not to park in spaces reserved for restaurants there.

You exit Middlebury on unpleasantly busy US 7 through a commercial area, the saving grace being the very wide shoulders. Turning off US 7, the route reaches Lake Dunmore and follows the western shore for several pleasant miles before passing through the town of Brandon. Shortly after leaving Brandon, VT 73 parallels Otter Creek for a couple of easy miles before you have a short, steep climb where the river turns away from the road. The short ride turns north for a direct return to Middlebury via Whiting and Cornwall, while the long option heads south to Sudbury before turning west and passing through Orwell on the way to the lake near Larrabees Point. The route then turns northeast to Shoreham, then Cornwall, and back to the start. Besides the two main loops that are described, partial cues are provided for options using Fernville Road, which heads west off VT 53 at the southern end of Lake Dunmore.

Note that VT 53 in the area of Lake Dunmore is actually busier on

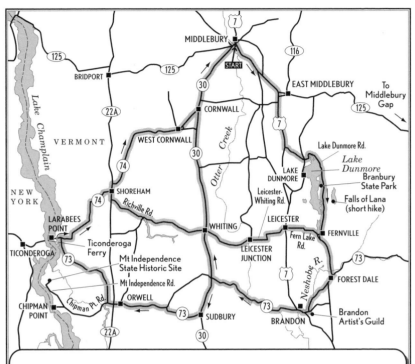

0.0	North on Main Street/VT 30 north/125 east
0.1	Right on Merchants Row-right around monument, right on South Pleasant Street
0.3	Right on Water Street just after forced left
0.7	Left at stop sign by high school
0.8	Right on US 7 south/VT 125 east
7.1	Left on VT 53 south for Lake Dunmore
8.6	Bear left with VT 53
13.9	Bear left with VT 53 S/Lake Dunmore Road (See text for Fernville Road options)
16.3	Bear left steeply uphill
16.5	Right on VT 73 west in Forest Dale
19.0	Right with VT 73 to Park Street
19.4	Straight with VT 73-US 7 joins from left
19.8	Bear left on VT 73 west
25.7	Left with VT 73 west at VT 30 *39-mile ride: Right on VT 30 north (continue with cues below)*

27.9	Right with VT 73 west
33.3	Cross VT 22A at flasher
39.1	Right on VT 74 east
43.7	Left with VT 74 at VT 22A north
44.2	Right with VT 74
51.6	Left on VT 30 north-VT 74 ends
53.1	Right with VT 30
55.8	Ilsley Public Library *39-mile ride*
28.4	Straight at Leicester-Whiting Road in Whiting
35.2	Straight with VT 30 in Cornwall
36.7	Right with VT 30
39.4	Ilsley Library

3. MIDDLEBURY-BRANDON

weekends than weekdays as it provides access to recreational areas. If riding this route on a summer weekend I would suggest an early start, which also means that US 7 will be less busy. For those who would like to combine an easy hike to a scenic waterfall with this tour, a short trail to the Falls of Lana starts from a trailhead parking area near Lake Dunmore.

0.0 Ride north on Main Street/VT 30 north/125 east.

0.1 Turn right on Merchants Row and bear right around the monument, then right on South Pleasant Street.

0.3 Turn right on Water Street just after the forced left.

0.7 Turn left at the stop sign by the high school.

0.8 Turn right on US 7 south/VT 125 east—moderate traffic, but good shoulder. *The next several miles are commercial strip and not particularly pleasant.*

1.9 Rosie's on the right is a good place for breakfast or lunch.

4.0 Straight with US 7 where VT 125 east turns left for Middlebury Gap. *Although there is still traffic, US 7 now enters open farm country.*

7.1 Turn left on VT 53 south for Lake Dunmore.

8.4 Turn left with VT 53 where West Shore Road is straight.

8.6 Bear left with VT 53 at Kampersville Deli.

8.9 There is a beach on the right that is likely private, but they might allow a passing cyclist a quick dip. Along the lake there is a 35-MPH speed limit that is generally respected by cars.

10.7 Branbury State Park is on the right. Swim here if you don't mind paying a fee.

11.1 Parking lot on the left with the trailhead for hiking trails to the Falls of Lana and Silver Lake. *It is an easy half-mile to the waterfalls and farther to the lake. Whether or not you have a lock, I suggest hiding your bike in the woods to avoid vandalism, which has been reported for cars here.*

13.9 Bear left with VT 53 S/Lake Dunmore Road where Fernville Road bears right.

For Fernville Road options: See the cues below.

16.3 Bear left steeply uphill where there's a side road right.

16.5 Turn right on VT 73 west in Forest Dale—Watroba's General Store is here.

18.1 Bear right with VT 73 where Country Club Road is left.

19.0 Turn right with VT 73 to Park Street in Brandon, which has many fine houses lining it.

Brandon was chartered in 1761 and soon became an important mill town with saw- and gristmills powered by the Neshobe River that flows through (and under) the center of town. Plentiful local deposits of iron ore contributed to the manufacturing of stoves and other iron products. When the Burlington-Rutland Railroad was constructed through town in 1849, the building of railroad cars became an important industry.

19.4 Straight with VT 73 where US 7 joins from the left.

19.5 The Brandon Artist's Guild is on the right with a good selection of locally produced arts and crafts.

If you're hungry, try Sully's Place on the left or Miss B's Kitchen on the right. The Brandon downtown area is showing signs of renewed vitality, although it is not as vigorous as Middlebury. In 2003 some 40 painted fiberglass pig sculptures were displayed around town. Although these were auctioned off that fall, visitors may still see some of them lurking about town.

19.8 Bear left on VT 73 west where US 7 bears right.

Just over a mile after leaving Brandon, Otter Creek appears on the left and the road follows it for a couple of pleasant miles.

23.5 Where Otter Creek turns right and the road leaves the river valley, you have a half-mile of steep climbing.

The sign at the top says 9 percent, but the middle section feels well over 10 percent to me—and my legs.

25.7 Turn left with VT 73 west where it joins VT 30 south—no shoulder, but generally light traffic.

For the 39-mile ride: Turn right on VT 30 north and continue with cues below.

A seriously winding road

27.7 A church with an interesting steeple is on the left.

27.9 Turn right with VT 73 west—rolling terrain for the next few miles, although mostly downhill.

32.9 Hawk's Country Kitchen is on the right in Orwell, and Buxton's Store is on the left.

Note: The tiny bank building on the left a little farther on—it's still in daily use and said to be the smallest in the country.

33.3 Cross VT 22A at the flasher.

33.7 Turn right with VT 73 west.

Chipman Point Road/VT 73A will take you to Mount Independence (named by the troops in honor of the new Declaration of Independence), a prominence rising across the lake from Fort Ticonderoga. Here American soldiers occupied fortifications from June 1776 until July the following year, when the site was abandoned in the face of a superior British advance. There is a visitors center and museum at the site, but getting there requires a long ride on a dead-end road.

37.7 As you turn right where the road approaches the lake, looking across you can clearly see the red roofs of Fort Ticonderoga.

39.1 Turn right on VT 74 east—the Ticonderoga ferry is to the left.
VT 74 makes a number of turns over the next several miles and in all cases follow the main road.

43.3 Right with VT 74 entering Shoreham.

43.7 Turn left with VT 74 at a T-intersection where it joins VT 22A north.

44.2 Turn right with VT 74.
You will gently climb to the top of a low ridge that offers alternating views of the Green Mountains to the right and the Adirondacks to the left.

49.9 Cross Bingham Street in West Cornwall—there are some fine houses on both sides of Bingham Street.

51.6 Turn left on VT 30 north at a T-intersection where VT 74 ends.

53.1 Bear right with VT 30.

55.2 The Middlebury College Museum of Art is on the right and should be open during the day.
There is bike parking in front of the building, or you should be able to bring your bike inside if you wish.

55.8 Ilsley Public Library—end of the tour.

39-MILE RIDE

28.4 Straight at Leicester—Whiting Road in Whiting.
For the next 2 miles you will have almost continuous views of the Green Mountains and the Adirondacks on either side.

35.2 Straight with VT 30 in Cornwall.
This is mile 51.6 above; finish with those cues.

FERNVILLE ROAD OPTIONS

These variations offer different views more than a greatly changed distance for the short ride. Cues are only provided for those segments that use different roads.

Option 1

13.9 Bear right on Fernville Road where VT 53 south bears left.

14.1 Turn right at a T-intersection on Fern Lake Road.

14.5 Bear left on Fern Lake Road where Hooker Road bears right.

16.1 Cross US 7 onto Leicester–Whiting Road in Leicester.

17.7 Right with Leicester–Whiting Road at a stop sign.

21.8 Turn right on VT 30 north at the stop sign in Whiting.
This is mile 28.4 on the short route above.

Option 2 (from above intersection)

21.8 Straight onto Shoreham–Whiting Road (becomes Richville Road in Addison County) at the stop sign in Whiting.

28.0 Turn right on US 7 north—moderate traffic, but good shoulder here.

28.9 Turn right with VT 74.
This is mile 44.2 on the long route above.

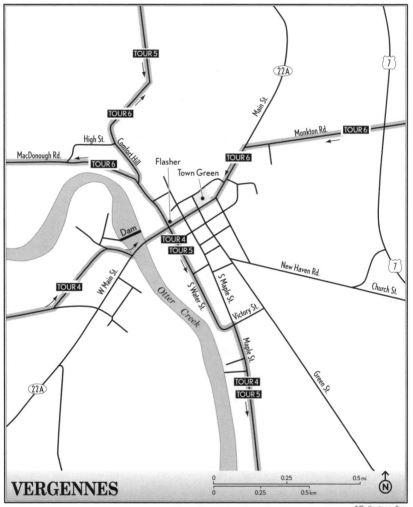

TOUR 5

TOUR 6

22A

7

Main St.

High St.

Comfort Hill

Monkton Rd.   TOUR 6

MacDonough Rd.   TOUR 6

Flasher

Town Green

TOUR 6

Dam

TOUR 4
TOUR 5

New Haven Rd.

7

Church St.

TOUR 4

W Main St.

S Water St.

S Maple St.

Victory St.

Otter Creek

Maple St.

22A

TOUR 4
TOUR 5

Green St.

0   0.25   0.5 mi
0   0.25   0.5 km

N

VERGENNES

© The Countryman Press

4

Middlebury–Vergennes

*Adirondack views, lake views,
and Morgan horses*

- **DISTANCE**: 49 or 62 miles
- **TERRAIN/DIFFICULTY**: Generally lightly to moderately rolling with flat riding near the lake; moderate.
- **START**: Main Street/VT 30/VT 125 at the Bike Center, on the opposite side from Ilsley Public Library in downtown Middlebury.
- **GETTING THERE/PARKING**: Middlebury isn't near an interstate, so your route there will depend on where you're coming from. It does lie on US 7, which is the major north-south road in western Vermont. There is public parking behind the library and on Bakery Lane, but be sure not to park in spaces reserved for restaurants.

This is an exceptionally pleasant ride with wonderful scenery, lightly rolling roads and very little traffic. Leaving Middlebury you soon pass many dairy farms and have excellent views of the Champlain Basin and the Adirondacks in the distance. Approaching the lake and the Chimney Point Bridge, you have an opportunity to visit historic sites in Vermont or in New York. There is an option to add 13 flat and pleasant miles from Vergennes, which is an attractive town and good midway lunch spot. You have lightly rolling roads through farming country all the way back to Middlebury, and pass by the Morgan Horse Farm near the end of the tour.

0.0 Ride south with Main Street/VT 125 west/VT 30.

0.0+ Turn right with VT 125 at College Street.

8.2 Turn right with VT 125 at a T-intersection joining VT 22A north in Bridport.

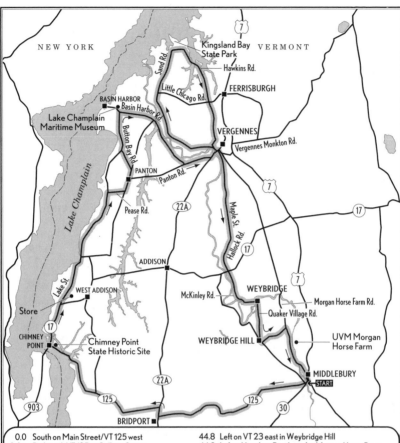

0.0	South on Main Street/VT 125 west
0.0+	Right with VT 125 at College Street
8.2	Right with VT 125 at VT 22A north in Bridport
8.7	Left with VT 125 west
15.6	Right onto VT 17 east in Chimney Point
17.7	Bear left on Lake Street at West Addison General Store
23.6	Right on Pease Road
24.4	Left onto Jersey Street (no sign)
25.5	Bear left onto Button Bay Road
28.3	Right onto Basin Harbor Road
32.7	Left onto Panton Road
33.9	Left onto West Street approaching Vergennes
34.2	Right onto Canal Street
34.3	Left on VT 22A; cross Otter Creek
34.5	Right onto Water Street (no sign) at flasher *Left for 62-mile ride (see cues below)*
35.0	Right on South Maple Street (later becomes Hallock Road) after forced left
40.5	Cross VT 17 to Mckinley Road (becomes Quaker Village Road) at flasher

44.8	Left on VT 23 east in Weybridge Hill
44.9	Left at Hamilton Road sign for Morgan Horse Farm
46.3	Right on Morgan Horse Farm Road
48.1	Bear left on Pulp Mill Bridge Road through bridge
48.2	Right on Seymour Street after bridge
48.7	Left with Seymour Street under railroad overpass, then an immediate right
49.0	Right on Main Street
49.2	Ilsley Library *Kingsland Bay option (62-mile ride)*
34.5	Left on Macdonough Drive at flasher
35.9	Right on Sand Road
44.8	Right on Botsford Road at Toppers Crossing Road
45.6	Bear left on Comfort Hill Road-High Street bears right
47.0	Left on Macdonough Drive (no sign) at stop sign
47.2	Cross VT 22A/Main Street to Water Street (no sign) at
47.4	flasher in Vergennes *This is mile 34.5 in main loop above; add 12.9 miles to following cues.*

4. MIDDLEBURY–VERGENNES

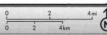

© The Countryman Press

8.7 Turn left with VT 125 west.

This view descending from Bridport is one of my favorites, particularly on a sunny morning; I always find it difficult not to smile when making the turn.

13.6 You have your first view of the elegant Chimney Point Bridge to the left.

14.6 Ride over a tree-lined causeway between the lake and a marsh.

In spring's high water, the lake is often lapping at the edge of the road or even flowing over it by a few inches.

15.6 Turn right on VT 17 east in Chimney Point.

OPTION 1

You can visit the museum at the Chimney Point State Historic Site on the left just before the bridge. This area got its name because after the British burned all of the French structures here, the chimneys were all that was left standing. The museum contains a number of exhibits on the early Native American and French settlers in this area. The museum is open Wednesday through Sunday, 9:30–5:00 PM from late May to mid-October (802-759-2412); admission fee.

OPTION 2

Ride across the Chimney Point Bridge and explore the old Crown Point fort (fee for museum; grounds and walking tour are free) before returning.

17.7 Bear left on Lake Street at West Addison General Store.

23.6 Bear right on Pease Road.

24.4 Turn left on Jersey Street (no sign) at a T-intersection.

25.5 Bear left on Button Bay Road.

28.3 Turn right onto Basin Harbor Road at a T-intersection.

32.7 Turn left onto Panton Road at a T-intersection.

33.9 Turn left onto West Street approaching Vergennes.

34.2 Turn right onto Canal Street at a T-intersection.

34.3 Turn left onto VT 22A at a T-intersection and cross Otter Creek.

Vergennes is Vermont's oldest city, established in 1788. The city's name was suggested by Ethan Allen to honor the Comte de Vergennes, who served as the French Minister of Foreign Affairs and supported American interests during the Revolution.

34.5 Turn right on Water Street (no sign) at the flasher.

OPTION 3

The main town and food are uphill—the town green is a good spot for lunch.

OPTION 4

Turn left here for the 62-mile ride; see the cues below.

35.0 Turn right on S. Maple Street (later becomes Hallock Road) after a forced left.

40.5 Carefully cross VT 17 to Mckinley Road (becomes Quaker Village Road) at the flasher.

There is a limited sight line to the left——you may want to dismount and walk across.

42.8 Cross Otter Creek at a dam in Weybridge.

44.8 Turn left on VT 23 east in Weybridge Hill.

44.9 Turn left on Hamilton Road signed for Morgan Horse Farm.

46.3 Turn right on Morgan Horse Farm Road at a T-intersection.

46.8 The UVM Morgan Horse Farm is on the left.

Visiting hours are 9:00–4:00 daily (tours on the hour), from May 1–October 31; admission fee.

Colonel Joseph Battell began breeding Morgans on his farm in Weybridge, just outside Middlebury, in the late 1800s. He was intensely interested in preserving and promoting America's first native breed of horse, and in 1906 he gave his farm and horses to the U.S. Government, which in 1951 turned it over to the University of Vermont. Colonel Battell was a philanthropist with many interests. During his lifetime he bought some of

Cyclists passing hay bales on VT 125 west of Middlebury

the most beautiful mountains—including Camel's Hump—in 14 towns of Vermont, and gave them to the people of Vermont to be held in trust by Middlebury College.

48.1 Bear left on Pulp Mill Bridge Road through the covered bridge.

48.2 Bear right on Seymour Street after the bridge.

48.7 Turn left with Seymour Street under the railroad overpass and then make an immediate right.

49.0 Turn right on Main Street at a T-intersection.

49.2 Ilsley Public Library—end of the tour

KINGSLAND BAY OPTION (62-MILE RIDE)

34.5 Turn left on Macdonough Drive at the flasher.

This street is named after Lieutenant Thomas Macdonough, who in 1814 was ordered to build a small fleet to defend Lake Champlain, specifically, "The object is to leave no doubt of your commanding the lake and the waters connected, and that in due time." This site was chosen over established shipbuilding towns on the lake because it was 7 miles up Otter Creek and thus considered less vulnerable to the British, who were busily building their own fleet on the Richelieu River. Vergennes was already a thriving industrial town by this time, with all the raw materials and facilities to work them that the young officer needed. As proof, the brig Saratoga *was built in 40 days that spring, followed by the schooner* Ticonderoga, *the brig* Eagle *(launched 17 days after the keel was laid), and six gunboats. This small fleet defeated the world's greatest naval power of the time in the Battle of Plattsburgh that autumn, with the event commemorated by the towering obelisk, erected in 1914, in downtown Plattsburgh.*

34.8 Small park on the left at Otter Creek landing.

35.9 Bear right on Sand Road where Walker Road is sharply right.

41.3 Turn right at Kingsland Bay State Park.

41.9 Forced right turn onto Hawkins Road.

42.7 Ride across a narrow causeway with water all around you—a very pretty spot.

44.8 Cross Little Chicago Road to Botsford Road at the stop sign.

45.6 Bear right on Botsford Road at Toppers Crossing Road.

47.0 Bear left on Comfort Hill Road where High Street bears right.
Caution: there is a hidden stop sign at the bottom of this hill.

47.2 Turn left on Macdonough Drive (no sign) at the stop sign.

47.4 Cross VT 22A/Main Street to Water Street (no sign) at the flasher in Vergennes.
This is mile 34.5 in the main loop above—add 12.9 miles to the following cues.

5

Middlebury–Burlington

*Historic college town to
Queen City and back*

- **DISTANCE**: 65 or 86 miles.
- **TERRAIN/DIFFICULTY**: Overall lightly rolling with more moderately rolling sections; moderately difficult with the direct return and moderate if done over two days.
- **START**: Ilsley Public Library, Main Street/VT 30/VT 125 in Middlebury, across from the Bike Center.
- **GETTING THERE/PARKING**: Middlebury isn't near an interstate, so your route there will depend on where you're coming from. It does lie on US 7, which is the major north-south road in western Vermont. There is public parking behind the library and some of it is designated as overnight spaces. There is also parking on Bakery Lane, but be sure not to park in spaces reserved for restaurants.

This tour is presented both as a point-to-point ride between Middlebury and downtown Burlington and return, as well as a shorter loop that doesn't go all the way into Burlington. Although strong riders could easily do the former as a day ride, with lunch in Burlington if they wished, for most riders it will work better as a two-day tour with an overnight there. (See the Burlington regional intro for information on lodging possibilities there.) The direct return route is planned as a challenging and satisfying day ride. There is an option to add about 8 flat miles near Vergennes on the way back to Middlebury.

This tour is planned to start in Middlebury, but there's no reason that you couldn't begin in Burlington. However, try not to start from Burlington during the week, as there is heavy local traffic during the morning and evening rush hours. A Middlebury start assumes midday or early afternoon arrival in Burlington, and I would suggest leaving

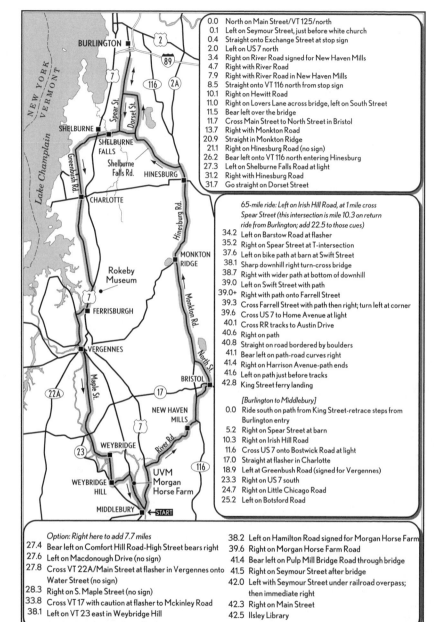

0.0	North on Main Street/VT 125/north
0.1	Left on Seymour Street, just before white church
0.4	Straight onto Exchange Street at stop sign
2.0	Left on US 7 north
3.4	Right on River Road signed for New Haven Mills
4.7	Right with River Road
7.9	Right with River Road in New Haven Mills
8.5	Straight onto VT 116 north from stop sign
10.1	Right on Hewitt Road
11.0	Right on Lovers Lane across bridge, left on South Street
11.5	Bear left over the bridge
11.7	Cross Main Street to North Street in Bristol
13.7	Right with Monkton Road
20.9	Straight in Monkton Ridge
21.1	Right on Hinesburg Road (no sign)
26.2	Bear left onto VT 116 north entering Hinesburg
27.3	Left on Shelburne Falls Road at light
31.2	Right with Hinesburg Road
31.7	Go straight on Dorset Street

*65-mile ride: Left on Irish Hill Road, at 1 mile cross
Spear Street (this intersection is mile 10.3 on return
ride from Burlington; add 22.5 to those cues)*

34.2	Left on Barstow Road at flasher
35.2	Right on Spear Street at T-intersection
37.6	Left on bike path at barn at Swift Street
38.1	Sharp downhill right turn-cross bridge
38.7	Right with wider path at bottom of downhill
39.0	Left on Swift Street with path
39.0+	Right with path onto Farrell Street
39.3	Cross Farrell Street with path then right; turn left at corner
39.6	Cross US 7 to Home Avenue at light
40.1	Cross RR tracks to Austin Drive
40.6	Right on path
40.8	Straight on road bordered by boulders
41.1	Bear left on path-road curves right
41.4	Right on Harrison Avenue-path ends
41.6	Left on path just before tracks
42.8	King Street ferry landing

[Burlington to Middlebury]

0.0	Ride south on path from King Street-retrace steps from Burlington entry
5.2	Right on Spear Street at barn
10.3	Right on Irish Hill Road
11.6	Cross US 7 onto Bostwick Road at light
17.0	Straight at flasher in Charlotte
18.9	Left at Greenbush Road (signed for Vergennes)
23.3	Right on US 7 south
24.7	Right on Little Chicago Road
25.2	Left on Botsford Road

Option: Right here to add 7.7 miles

27.4	Bear left on Comfort Hill Road-High Street bears right
27.6	Left on Macdonough Drive (no sign)
27.8	Cross VT 22A/Main Street at flasher in Vergennes onto Water Street (no sign)
28.3	Right on S. Maple Street (no sign)
33.8	Cross VT 17 with caution at flasher to Mckinley Road
38.1	Left on VT 23 east in Weybridge Hill
38.2	Left on Hamilton Road signed for Morgan Horse Farm
39.6	Right on Morgan Horse Farm Road
41.4	Bear left on Pulp Mill Bridge Road through bridge
41.5	Right on Seymour Street after bridge
42.0	Left with Seymour Street under railroad overpass; then immediate right
42.3	Right on Main Street
42.5	Ilsley Library

5. MIDDLEBURY–BURLINGTON

there after 9 AM, although the bike path helps in avoiding traffic. In some years a summer tourist train has traveled between these two places, and twice I've ridden it south (with my bike aboard) in the morning and then cycled back after a pleasant lunch in Middlebury.

MIDDLEBURY TO BURLINGTON

After a few miles on US 7 leaving town, you turn off onto lightly rolling side roads for New Haven Mills, following the New Haven River. Level riding on VT 116 follows, then a turn east to the town of Bristol. Very lightly rolling terrain in a farming valley brings you to Monkton Ridge, where things change dramatically. A long descent leads to 5 miles of steeply rolling riding to Hinesburg, where there is a return to more level riding on the way to Shelburne and the approach to Burlington. The actual entry to the city is achieved via the pleasant lakefront bicycle path.

0.0 Ride north on Main Street/VT 125/VT 30 east.

The stone bridge you immediately cross has an interesting history. The town fathers proposed an iron bridge for this site after the original wooden bridge burned down. Philanthropist Joseph Battell was so adamant that a stone bridge would last longer and be of more benefit to the town that he paid for the difference in cost himself. To your right as you approach Merchants Row is the Battell Block, the largest commercial building downtown.

0.1 Turn left on Seymour Street, just before the handsome white Congregational Church, with its magnificent multitiered steeple.

0.4 Continue straight onto Exchange Street at the stop sign.

2.0 Turn left on US 7 north, which has moderate traffic but also a wide shoulder.

2.5 On the right is a barn with large lettering for "Euclide Quesnel Dairy Cows."

The Quesnels must be a large farming family, as their name is associated with other farms in the Middlebury area.

3.4 Turn right on River Road signed for New Haven Mills.

4.7 Bear right on River Road.

7.9 Bear right on River Road in New Haven Mills.

8.5 Ride straight onto VT 116 north from the stop sign.

10.1 Turn right on Hewitt Road.

10.7 There is a wonderful house with gingerbread eves on the left.

11.0 Bear right on Lovers Lane and cross the bridge, then turn left on South Street.

11.5 Bear left over the bridge (as of summer 2003 this bridge is closed to cars but open for bikes).

11.7 Cross Main Street to North Street in Bristol—the town green is on the left and shops are to the right.

I was once riding in the area with friends and we made a coffee stop in town. On the board listing the specialty drinks, the last item named "Why Bother?" caught my eye—it was decaf espresso with skim milk.

13.3 There is a "penny farthing" (high-wheel bicycle) sculpture on the yellow barn to the left.

13.7 Turn right with Monkton Road.

The next 7 miles of riding are lightly rolling through farm country, with almost continuous views of the Green Mountains to your right.

19.2 There is a very unusual octagonal silo on the right made of stacked two-by-fours.

20.9 Ride straight in Monkton Ridge where there's a general store.

21.1 Bear right on Hinesburg Road (no sign).

The road ahead is seriously rolling for the next 5 miles.

26.2 Bear left at the wye onto VT 116 north entering Hinesburg.

27.3 Turn left on Shelburne Falls Road at the light.

31.2 Turn right with Hinesburg Road.

31.7 Go straight on Dorset Hill Road.

FOR 65-MILE RIDE

Turn left on Irish Hill Road here and in 1.1 miles cross Spear Street. That intersection is mile 10.3 on the return ride from Burlington—add 22.5 to those cues.

34.2 Turn left on Barstow Road at the flasher.

35.2 Turn right on Spear Street at a T-intersection.

36.8 Overlook Park on left, which has great views of the Lake Champlain Basin and the Adirondacks, especially late in the day.

37.6 Turn left on the bike path at a white barn just before the traffic light at Swift Street.

Option: *You can stay straight on Spear Street for a less complex but busier route to downtown Burlington. This is recommended if you were doing this as an overnight tour and staying in one of the motels on US 2. Although it requires some navigation, the bike path is scenic and obviously has less (car) traffic. See the cues at bottom for the Spear Street route.*

38.1 Make a very sharp downhill right turn with the bike path, after which you cross a wooden bridge, which can be dangerous when wet.

38.7 Turn right with the wider path at the bottom of the downhill.

39.0 Turn left on Swift Street with the bike path.

39.0+ Turn right with the path onto Farrell Street.

39.3 Cross Farrell Street with the path and turn right, then left at the corner.

39.6 Cross US 7 to Home Avenue at the light.

40.1 Cross the RR tracks to Austin Drive.

40.6 Turn right on the bike path.

40.8 Ride straight on the road bordered by boulders.
There is a side path to a rocky beach on the left, with pavilions and restrooms nearby.

41.1 Bear left on the bike path where the road curves right.

A young girl inspects some strange cargo in Bristol

41.4 Turn right on Harrison Avenue when the bike path ends.

41.6 Turn left on the bike path just before the tracks.

42.5 Note the carved white boulders along the shore at a small peninsular park.

42.8 King Street ferry landing—end of the northern ride.

BURLINGTON-MIDDLEBURY

Leave Burlington as you entered it, riding on the bike path and Spear Street. Turning west in Shelburne, you will soon cycle near the lake and on to Charlotte. You have easy riding on mostly side roads all the way to Vergennes, which is a possible lunch stop. Lightly rolling roads in farm country bring you to Weybridge Hill and then past the Morgan Horse Farm on your return to Middlebury.

0.0 South on bike path from King Street.

Retrace your steps from the Burlington entry.

5.2 Turn right on Spear Street by the white barn, or continue on Spear Street if coming from the motels on US 2.

10.3 Turn right on Irish Hill Road—fast downhill ahead.

11.2 Shelburne Falls—general store on the right.

11.6 Cross US 7 onto Bostwick Road at the light.

15.4 Continue straight with Greenbush Road where Lake Road is on the right.

Option: *Lake Road to Ferry Road (turn left) to Charlotte is very attractive if you don't mind 2 more miles of riding.*

17.0 Continue straight at the flasher in Charlotte.

The Old Brick Store is on the left with a wonderful funky clock on the side wall, which they sell good quality note cards of.

18.9 Turn left with Greenbush Road (signed for Vergennes).

21.2 Straight with Greenbush Road where Stage Road is left.

If you want to climb Mount Philo for the view (see tour 6), turn left here.

23.3 Turn right on US 7 south, which can be busy but has a good shoulder here.

23.4 The Rokeby Museum is on the left (http://www.rokeby.org/home.html—admission fee).

The Robinson family lived here through four generations and some 170 years. They were Quaker millers, farmers, abolitionists, authors, naturalists, and artists; besides their personal story this museum documents the social history of Vermont from the 1790s to 1961.

Rokeby Museum is one of the best-documented Underground Railroad sites in the country and is designated a National Historic Landmark.

24.7 Turn right on Little Chicago Road.

24.9 Bear left, now on Depot Road, and ride over a small gorge.

25.0 Caution—cross the angled RR track carefully.

25.2 Turn left on Botsford Road.
Option: *Turn right here to add 7.7 flat and pleasant miles with the Kingsland Bay extension—see the cues below.*

26.0 Bear right with Botsford Road at Toppers Crossing Road.

27.4 Bear left on Comfort Hill Road where High Street bears right.
Caution—there is a hidden stop sign at the bottom of the hill.

27.6 Turn left on Macdonough Drive (no sign) at a T-intersection.

27.8 Cross VT 22A/Main Street at the flasher in Vergennes onto Water Street (no sign).
Option: *The main town and food are uphill to the left.*

28.3 Turn right on S. Maple Street (no sign) after forced left.

33.8 Caution—Cross VT 17 at the flasher to McKinley Road with great care.
There is a limited sight line to the left—you may want to dismount and walk across.

36.1 Cross Otter Creek at a dam in Weybridge.

38.1 Turn left on VT 23 east in Weybridge Hill.

38.2 Turn left on Hamilton Road signed for Morgan Horse Farm.

39.6 Turn right on Morgan Horse Farm Road at a T-intersection.

40.1 The UVM Morgan Horse Farm is on the left.
Visiting hours are 9–4 daily (tours on the hour), from May 1–October 31; admission fee.
Colonel Joseph Battell began breeding Morgans on his farm in Weybridge, just outside Middlebury, in the late 1800s. He was intensely interested in preserving and promoting America's first native breed of horse, and in 1906 he gave his farm and Morgan

horses to the U. S. Government, which in 1951 turned them over to the University of Vermont. Colonel Battell was a philanthropist with many interests. During his lifetime he bought some of the most beautiful mountains—including Camel's Hump—in 14 towns of Vermont, and gave them to the people of Vermont to be held in trust by Middlebury College.

41.4 Bear left on Pulp Mill Bridge Road through the covered bridge.

41.5 Bear right on Seymour Street after the bridge.

42.0 Turn left with Seymour Street under the railroad overpass and then make an immediate right.

42.3 Turn right on Main Street at a T-intersection.

42.5 Ilsley Public Library—end of the tour.

OPTIONAL ROAD-ONLY ENTRY TO BURLINGTON, AVOIDING BIKE PATH

37.2 Cross Swift Street at the light.

39.4 Turn left on US 2 west/Main Street from the "rotary" at the University of Vermont campus. (Note: Turn right on US 2 east for lodging.)

40.4 Great view of the city and lake coming downhill—especially close to sunset.

41.1 Turn left on Battery Street (or right for the Radisson Hotel).

41.3 King Street ferry landing.

KINGSLAND BAY OPTION

25.2 Turn right on Hawkins Road.

27.2 Ride across a narrow causeway with water all around you—a very pretty spot.

28.7 Turn left on Sand Road at Kingsland Bay State Park.

34.2 Bear left with Sand Road where Walker Road is sharply left.

35.3 Small park on the right at Otter Creek landing.

35.6 Cross VT 22A/Main Street at the flasher in Vergennes to Water Street (no sign).

This is mile 28.8 from Burlington or 50.5 on the direct return—add 7.8 miles to the remaining cues.

BURLINGTON AND THE VERMONT CENTRAL TOURS

A funky clock on the wall of the Old Brick Store in Charlotte

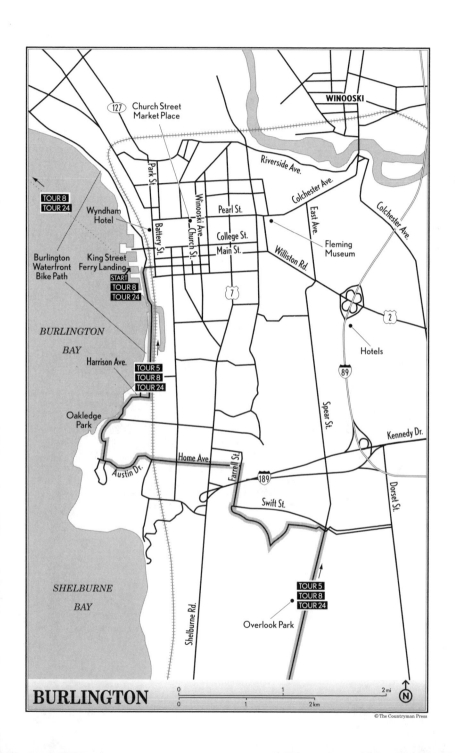

Church Street
Market Place

WINOOSKI

127

Riverside Ave.

Park St.

Colchester Ave.

Colchester Ave.

TOUR 8
TOUR 24

Winooski Ave.

Pearl St.

East Ave.

Wyndham
Hotel

Battery St.

Church St.

College St.

Fleming
Museum

Main St.

Burlington
Waterfront
Bike Path

King Street
Ferry Landing

Williston Rd.

START
TOUR 8
TOUR 24

7

BURLINGTON
BAY

2

Hotels

Harrison Ave.

TOUR 5
TOUR 8
TOUR 24

89

Oakledge
Park

Kennedy Dr.

Home Ave.

Farrell St.

Austin Dr.

189

Swift St.

Spear St.

Dorset St.

SHELBURNE
BAY

Shelburne Rd.

TOUR 5
TOUR 8
TOUR 24

Overlook Park

BURLINGTON

0   1   2 mi
0   1   2 km

N

© The Countryman Press

BURLINGTON IS BY FAR Vermont's largest city, and it has grown tremendously over the last decade. Unfortunately, not all of that growth has been positive, as many of the area's best cycling roads have suffered heavily increased traffic, particularly during commuting hours. However, there is still excellent riding available in the area, including the city's delightful lakeside bike path. The city is wonderfully situated, sloping down to the always-active lakefront with the Adirondacks in the distance. Sunset on a clear summer evening can be truly spectacular.

Burlington was incorporated in 1864, when the original village was divided into the City of Burlington and the town of South Burlington. The latter is generally an unfriendly place for cyclists, with large strip mall developments along US Highways 2 and 7. The tours in this book that pass through South Burlington use the routes that are considered the best by local cyclists. Burlington itself is a fascinating city with a long and rich history, architecturally distinguished neighborhoods, and a strong cultural scene. In the late 1970s, several downtown blocks became the Church Street Marketplace, which is a vibrant pedestrian mall with shops, cafés, eateries, and sidewalk entertainers.

Attractions in town include the ECHO (Ecology, Culture and History and Opportunities) Lake Aquarium and Science Center on the waterfront, near the Burlington Boathouse at the foot of College Street. The University of Vermont's Fleming Museum on Colchester Avenue features primitive art collections and American art from the past two centuries. The Shelburne Museum is several miles south of the city and is often described as a collection of collections, with Americana of all sorts housed across sprawling grounds, but also including the paddle wheeler *Ticonderoga,* which was dramatically hauled to the site from the nearby lake, whose waters she long plied.

The only hotel in the downtown area is the Wyndham Burlington at 60 Battery Street (802-658-6500), although there are inns and B&Bs available, many of them up the hill near the UVM campus. Other large hotels are located at the I-89/US 2 interchange and more traditional motels are on US 2 in the airport area. Church Street Marketplace is a great place to find something to eat, although there are other restaurants grouped near the waterfront. Burlington probably has more interesting dining options for a city its size than anywhere else in the country. Whenever I'm in town I always make a point of having a pint of the excellent Smoked Porter at the Vermont Brewing Company.

Tourism Info

The Lake Champlain Chamber of Commerce, 60 Main Street, Burlington, 05401 (877-686-5253 or www.vermont.org)

Bike Shops

Burlington—Ski Rack, 85 Main Street (802-658-3313)

Burlington—North Star Cyclery, 100 Main Street (802-863-3832)

Richmond—Village Bicycle Repair, 4 W. Main Street (802-434-4876)

Shelburne—Climb High, 1861 Shelburne Road/US 7 (802-985-5055)

South Burlington—Earl's Cyclery & Fitness, 2500 Williston Road (866-327-5725)

6

Charlotte Loops

Farms, rolling hills, and distant views

- **DISTANCE:** 15, 25, 34, or 42 miles.
- **TERRAIN/DIFFICULTY:** The 15-mile loop is lightly rolling while the other rides are moderately rolling; the short ride is easy and the longer ones are moderately difficult.
- **START:** The Old Brick Store in Charlotte—note the funky clock on the sidewall. The store sells a note card with an excellent photo of this clock.
- **GETTING THERE/PARKING:** VT 7 to Ferry Road (VT F5), signed for Charlotte and the ferry to NY State. Limited parking across from the store, check with them about parking in their lot or elsewhere in town.

These rides south of Burlington pass some signs of the creeping expansion of the city's reach, while most of the countryside you ride through remains refreshingly rural. The short loop has a fairly easy time of it, while the longer rides involve substantial ups and downs. Any of these rides can be combined with tour 19 by taking the Charlotte—Essex ferry across the lake. Doing this would provide an all-day ride of 40–77 miles, with excellent scenery on both sides of the lake.

Charlotte, chartered in 1762, occupies hills and ridges overlooking Lake Champlain. As described in *Vermont Magazine,* Charlotte shoulders "its way between the glitzy refinement of Shelburne to the north and the blue-collar panache of Ferrisburgh to the south, trying to find a happy medium between the two extremes, and forging its own peculiar character in the process. This is a town dominated by rural landscapes, by farmland, hills, and orchard; it is also—quietly, to be sure—

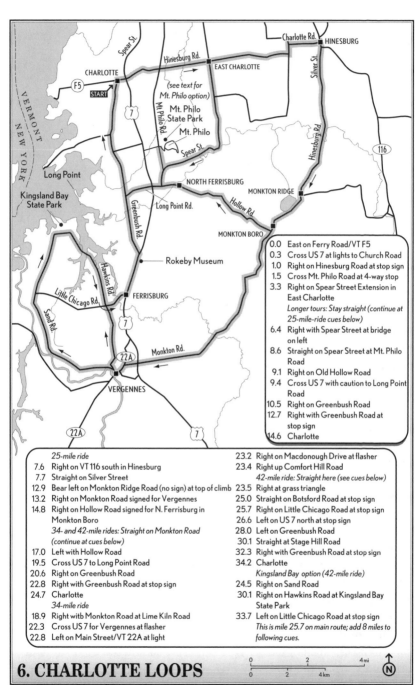

0.0	East on Ferry Road/VT F5
0.3	Cross US 7 at lights to Church Road
1.0	Right on Hinesburg Road at stop sign
1.5	Cross Mt. Philo Road at 4-way stop
3.3	Right on Spear Street Extension in East Charlotte
	Longer tours: Stay straight (continue at 25-mile-ride cues below)
6.4	Right with Spear Street at bridge on left
8.6	Straight on Spear Street at Mt. Philo Road
9.1	Right on Old Hollow Road
9.4	Cross US 7 with caution to Long Point Road
10.5	Right on Greenbush Road
12.7	Right with Greenbush Road at stop sign
14.6	Charlotte

25-mile ride

7.6	Right on VT 116 south in Hinesburg
7.7	Straight on Silver Street
12.9	Bear left on Monkton Ridge Road (no sign) at top of climb
13.2	Right on Monkton Road signed for Vergennes
14.8	Right on Hollow Road signed for N. Ferrisburg in Monkton Boro
	34- and 42-mile rides: Straight on Monkton Road (continue at cues below)
17.0	Left with Hollow Road
19.5	Cross US 7 to Long Point Road
20.6	Right on Greenbush Road
22.8	Right with Greenbush Road at stop sign
24.7	Charlotte

34-mile ride

18.9	Right with Monkton Road at Lime Kiln Road
22.3	Cross US 7 for Vergennes at flasher
22.8	Left on Main Street/VT 22A at light

23.2	Right on Macdonough Drive at flasher
23.4	Right up Comfort Hill Road
	42-mile ride: Straight here (see cues below)
23.5	Right at grass triangle
25.0	Straight on Botsford Road at stop sign
25.7	Right on Little Chicago Road at stop sign
26.6	Left on US 7 north at stop sign
28.0	Left on Greenbush Road
30.1	Straight at Stage Hill Road
32.3	Right with Greenbush Road at stop sign
34.2	Charlotte
	Kingsland Bay option (42-mile ride)
24.5	Right on Sand Road
30.1	Right on Hawkins Road at Kingsland Bay State Park
33.7	Left on Little Chicago Road at stop sign
	This is mile 25.7 on main route; add 8 miles to following cues.

6. CHARLOTTE LOOPS

0   2   4 mi
0   2   4 km

N

part and parcel of Vermont's Gold Coast. Small farms and modest homes are here, as they have always been; but they often sit cheek and jowl with more stately mansions." I've noticed a lot of construction in Charlotte village over the past two years and it looks like the town is moving closer to Shelburne, refinement wise.

After crossing US 7, there is rolling terrain all the way to Hinesburg and then on to Monkton Ridge for the longer loops. From there it is largely downhill and lightly rolling for the remainder of the tour. All loops have the option of visiting Mount Philo State Park and climbing to the summit for a commanding view of the surrounding countryside, with the lake and the Adirondacks making a fine backdrop. The two longer loops pass through Vergennes (see tour 5), which is a great spot for lunch or a break.

0.0 Ride east on Ferry Road/VT F5.

0.3 Cross US 7 at the lights to Church Road.

1.0 Turn right on Hinesburg Road at the stop sign.
The Charlotte Memorial Museum is on the left at the turn and has a small collection of local historical artifacts.

1.5 Cross Mount Philo Road at a 4-way stop.

3.3 Turn right on Spear Street Extension in East Charlotte.
For all longer tours stay straight here and continue at the 25-mile ride cues below.

6.4 Turn right with Spear Street where there's a covered bridge to the left.

8.6 Stay straight on Spear Street at Mount Philo Road.
Option: *Turn right here for a great view of the lake from Mount Philo Road or to climb to the top of Mount Philo. See the Mount Philo info at the end of this tour.*

9.1 Turn right on Old Hollow Road at a T-intersection.

9.4 Cross US 7 with caution to Long Point Road (also signed as Stage Road).

10.5 Turn right on Greenbush Road at a T-intersection.

12.7 Turn right with Greenbush Road at a stop sign.

14.6 Charlotte—end of the tour.

25-MILE RIDE

7.6 Turn right on VT 116 south at a T-intersection in Hinesburg.

7.7 Continue straight on Silver Street—the next 4 miles are seriously rolling.

11.9 Start of a mile-long climb to Monkton Ridge.

12.9 Bear left on Monkton Ridge Road (no sign) at the top of the climb.

13.1 Monkton Ridge—Monkton General Store on the left.

13.2 Bear right on Monkton Road signed for Vergennes, with a view of the Adirondacks over Cedar Lake to your right.

14.8 Turn right on Hollow Road signed for N. Ferrisburg in Monkton Boro. For the 34- and 42-mile rides: *Stay straight on Monkton Road and continue at the cues below.*

17.0 Turn left with Hollow Road.

17.8 Start of a downhill that becomes steep entering North Ferrisburg.

18.7 North Ferrisburg—a very sweet little village off the main track. *Blue Seal Feed is on the left at the bridge and was surely once a mill. Gargoyles are on the gateposts to the left after passing Vermont Studio Furniture.*

19.1 Option: Turn right here for a great view of the lake from Mount Philo Road or to climb to the top of Mount Philo. See the Mount Philo info at the end of this tour.

19.5 Cross US 7 with caution to Long Point Road (also signed as Stage Road).

20.6 Turn right on Greenbush Road at a T-intersection.

22.8 Turn right with Greenbush Road at a stop sign.

24.7 Charlotte—end of the tour.

34-MILE RIDE

18.9 Bear right on Monkton Road at Lime Kiln Road.

22.3 Cross US 7 for Vergennes at the flasher.

The sweeping panorama of the Champlain Basin from the summit of Mount Philo

22.8 Turn left on Main Street/VT 22A at the light.

23.1 The town green on the right makes a good lunch/rest spot. There are a number of food options nearby.

23.2 Turn right on Macdonough Drive at the flasher.

23.4 Bear right up Comfort Hill Road at the bottom of the hill.
For 42-mile ride: *Stay straight here and see the cues below.*

23.5 Bear right at a small grass triangle.

25.0 Stay straight on Botsford Road at the stop sign.

25.7 Turn right on Little Chicago Road at the stop sign.

26.3 Cross the angled RR track with caution—there is a small gorge just past this.

26.6 Turn left on US 7 north at the stop sign—there can be traffic here, but also a good wide shoulder.

27.8 The Rokeby Museum is on the right (see info in tour 5).

28.0 Turn left on Greenbush Road.
If traffic is busy enough that you can't cross both lanes at once, I recommend waiting in the shoulder to cross instead of the middle of the road.

30.1 Stay straight at Stage Hill Road.
Mount Philo option: Turn right here and cross US 7 to Old Hollow Road, then turn left on Mount Philo Road. See the Mount Philo info at the end of this tour.

32.3 Turn right with Greenbush Road at a stop sign.

34.2 Charlotte—end of the tour.

42-MILE RIDE/KINGSLAND BAY OPTION

23.5 Small park on the left at Otter Creek landing.

24.5 Bear right on Sand Road where Walker Road is sharply right.

30.1 Turn right on Hawkins Road at Kingsland Bay State Park.

31.6 Narrow causeway with water all around you—a very pretty spot.
This is a special place to me. I encourage you to get off your bike, if only for a minute or two, and listen to the birds and savor the privilege of being here. I've seen several great blue herons here.

33.7 Turn left on Little Chicago Road at the stop sign.
This is mile 25.7 on the main route—add 8 miles to the following cues.

MOUNT PHILO OPTION

The views of the Champlain Basin from the top of Mount Philo (elevation 968 feet) are exceptional, particularly late in the day with the sun setting over the Adirondacks. As you are only a few miles from the end of the ride, you could even stay for sunset and return to Charlotte before dark. Vermont was heavily glaciated and as the glaciers retreated northward, Mount Philo became an island in an inland sea, as evidenced by the marine sand deposits at its base. The Charlotte Whale, an 11,000-year-old beluga whale discovered in 1849 during railroad construction, is believed to have died in a shallow marsh of the Champlain Sea. Mount Philo State Park, created in 1924, is Vermont's oldest. The mile-long road to the summit is steep and twisting and there is a $2 charge for the pleasure/challenge of riding it.

Directions from Old Hollow Road and Mount Philo Road *(see detail map)*.

0.0 Ride north on Mount Philo Road.

0.5 Continue straight on Mount Philo Road where Spear Street turns right.

1.4 The park entrance is on the right.

Leaving the park, you can return to your route the way you came. There is also an option that saves some 3 miles of riding at the cost of a mile on a dirt road. For this option, ride straight onto State Park Road leaving the park.

1.4 Ride west on State Park Road.

2.0 Turn right on US 7 north at a T-intersection.

2.3 Turn left with caution on Thompsons Point Road (dirt).

If traffic is busy enough that you can't cross both lanes at once, I recommend waiting in the shoulder to cross instead of the middle of the road.

3.5 Turn right on Greenbush Road at a T-intersection.

3.5+ Right with Greenbush Road at a stop sign.

5.4 Charlotte—end of the tour.

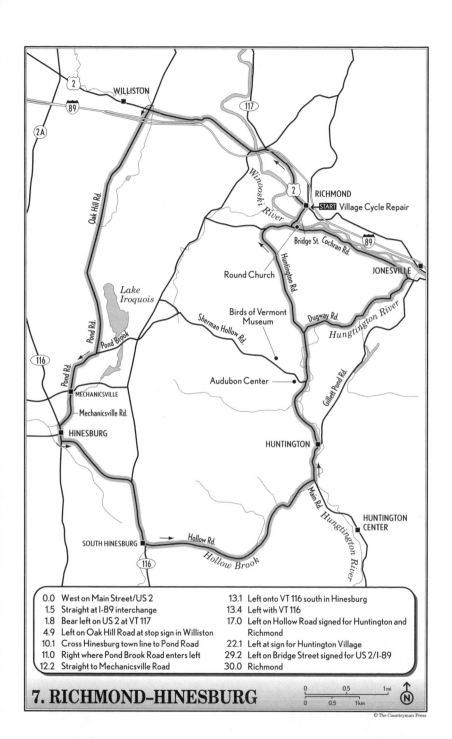

0.0	West on Main Street/US 2
1.5	Straight at I-89 interchange
1.8	Bear left on US 2 at VT 117
4.9	Left on Oak Hill Road at stop sign in Williston
10.1	Cross Hinesburg town line to Pond Road
11.0	Right where Pond Brook Road enters left
12.2	Straight to Mechanicsville Road
13.1	Left onto VT 116 south in Hinesburg
13.4	Left with VT 116
17.0	Left on Hollow Road signed for Huntington and Richmond
22.1	Left at sign for Huntington Village
29.2	Left on Bridge Street signed for US 2/I-89
30.0	Richmond

7. RICHMOND–HINESBURG

0   0.5   1mi
0   0.5   1km

N

© The Countryman Press

Richmond–Hinesburg

*Four-town tango—quiet river valleys
and a round church*

- **DISTANCE:** 30 miles.

- **TERRAIN/DIFFICULTY:** Generally lightly rolling with a few short, steeper climbs; moderate.

- **START:** Corner of Bridge and Main Streets/US 2 in Richmond. Village Bicycle Repair is located at this intersection (802-434-4876). Toscano Cafe & Bistro nearby has good food and the Bridge Street Café is across the street—be sure to check out the flood photographs in their front windows.

- **GETTING THERE/PARKING:** I-89 Exit 11, US 2 East for 1.5 miles to Richmond. Free parking in town center.

The area southeast of Burlington has seen intense growth in the past decade, lessening the appeal of some formerly bicycle-friendly roads in what had traditionally been farming country. However, it is still possible to find pleasant roads with light traffic and good views of the surrounding countryside and distant mountain ranges. Much of this ride follows streams and rivers in quiet valleys using roads that have been largely untouched by expanding suburbia.

The tour starts by heading northwest on US 2 to Williston, then drops south through Hinesburg, turns east to Huntington and finally north back to the start. There is an option near the end of the tour to visit the Huntington Gorge via some riding on a dirt road; see the information in the cues. Near the end of the ride you can visit the well-known Old Round Church in Richmond.

0.0 Ride west on Main Street/US 2—there can be some traffic here, but there is a shoulder after you leave town and things get much better after the I-89/VT 117 interchange.

1.5 Continue straight at the I-89 interchange (as if any cyclist in their right mind wouldn't?).

1.8 Bear left on US 2 at VT 117.

2.0 US 2 passes through a handsome and graceful arch bridge over the Winooski (Native American for "onion") River.

3.2 Start of the .7-mile climb up French Hill, with a welcome break and lesser grades halfway up.

4.9 Turn left on Oak Hill Road at the stop sign in Williston. The next 2.5 miles are rolling.

5.9 As you gain the eastern slope of a ridge, you get your initial view of Camel's Hump to the left and Mount Mansfield is behind your left shoulder.

7.5 End of the most serious climbing for the tour.

10.1 You're now on Pond Road as you cross the Hinesburg town line.

11.0 Turn right where Pond Brook Road enters left. Start of a downhill that is steep at times.

1.6 You might need to brake for a fairly sharp left on Pond Road. If you're going slowly enough to appreciate it, there's a view of the Adirondacks ahead just before this turn.

12.2 Go straight to Mechanicsville Road at an unusual intersection where all four roads have different names.

13.1 Turn left onto VT 116 south at a T-intersection in Hinesburg.

13.4 Turn left with VT 116.

17.0 Turn left on Hollow Road signed for Huntington and Richmond, with a store at the turn.

I discovered this delightful byway while developing a Burlington to Montpelier route for

Racing team training on Hinesburg Road near Richmond

a group tour, and it remains one of my favorite riding roads in the Burlington area. The road climbs gradually along a stream in a very small valley to a marsh at the top and then gently descends along another stream. Look for beaver dams and lodges on the way up and at the top.

21.9 There's an impressive collection of license plates to the left, but don't try to steal one!

22.1 Turn left at the T-intersection signed for Huntington Village.

22.5 The Huntington River appears far below you on the right.

22.9 Bear left with the main road at Huntington Village green as you come around a corner.

There are two country stores in town and the green would be a good place for lunch or a break.

23.6 As you leave Huntington Village there's a thick woods with a lush fern floor on the left. Soon the Huntington River appears on the right and you ride in its valley for the next 2 miles.

24.7 Located on Sherman Hollow Road to the left are an Audubon Center and the Birds of Vermont Museum.

25.8 Dugway Road turns right here along with the river and you have just over a mile of rolling terrain ahead. However, after the final crest there is a most enjoyable 2-mile descent into Richmond.

Option: *If you don't mind riding on some dirt, you can take Dugway Road to Huntington Gorge. However, don't even think of swimming there as many have died in the treacherous drops, as documented on a nearby memorial. Continue on Dugway Road and turn left on Cochran Road (paved) in Jonesville, which will bring you to the intersection at 29.2, where you turn right. This option adds about 3 miles.*

29.2 Turn left on Bridge Street signed for US 2/I-89.

29.4 Richmond's historic Old Round Church is on the right and may be open.

30.0 Richmond—end of the tour.

8

Burlington–Essex

The two-ferry, two-state tour

- **DISTANCE:** 42 or 50 miles.

- **TERRAIN/DIFFICULTY:** Moderately rolling; moderately difficult.

- **START:** Burlington ferry landing at King Street (cues start at Port Kent ferry landing).

- **GETTING THERE/PARKING:** I-89 to Exit 14, US 2 west to Battery Street, left one block to King Street and the ferry. There are parking lots along the waterfront, although they generally charge. You may find free on-street parking in residential neighborhoods near the downtown area.

This loop provides a chance to explore the eastern edge of the Adirondacks while using two ferries to cross the lake for the loop. Leaving the Port Kent ferry landing in New York, the route climbs away from the lake on backroads, with some additional climbing on NY 22 before starting the long descent into Willsboro. You can follow 22 directly to the return ferry in the historic village of Essex, or add 8.5 miles through Whallonsburg with fantastic views and excellent lakeshore riding. Back in Vermont, pleasant riding through Charlotte takes you to Shelburne, then on to Spear Street and the waterfront bike path into Burlington. Note: There is an 82-mile ride that uses these same ferries but gets much deeper into the Adirondacks; see tour 24 for this option.

Some local cyclists favor doing this ride in the opposite direction, but I prefer it this way for a number of reasons. Since the Burlington ferry crossing is a longer trip and scheduled less frequently, I like taking it in the morning when I can more easily predict my arrival there. Also, if you have to wait for a ferry, Essex (see p. 163) is a far nicer and

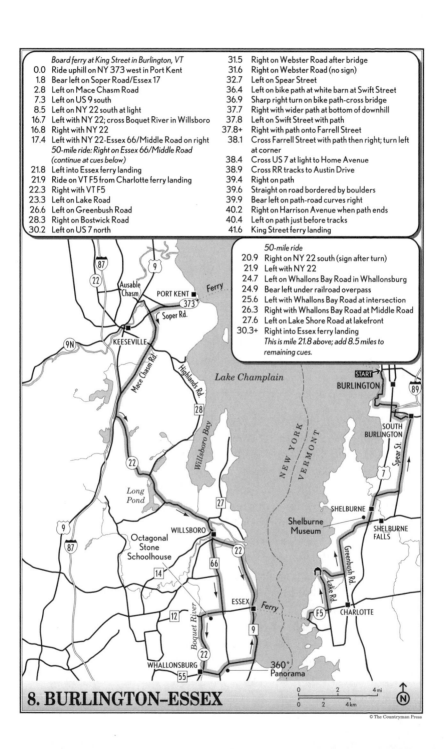

Board ferry at King Street in Burlington, VT

0.0	Ride uphill on NY 373 west in Port Kent
1.8	Bear left on Soper Road/Essex 17
2.8	Left on Mace Chasm Road
7.3	Left on US 9 south
8.5	Left on NY 22 south at light
16.7	Left with NY 22; cross Boquet River in Willsboro
16.8	Right with NY 22
17.4	Left with NY 22-Essex 66/Middle Road on right
	50-mile ride: Right on Essex 66/Middle Road (continue at cues below)
21.8	Left into Essex ferry landing
21.9	Ride on VT F5 from Charlotte ferry landing
22.3	Right with VT F5
23.3	Left on Lake Road
26.6	Left on Greenbush Road
28.3	Right on Bostwick Road
30.2	Left on US 7 north

31.5	Right on Webster Road after bridge
31.6	Right on Webster Road (no sign)
32.7	Left on Spear Street
36.4	Left on bike path at white barn at Swift Street
36.9	Sharp right turn on bike path-cross bridge
37.7	Right with wider path at bottom of downhill
37.8	Left on Swift Street with path
37.8+	Right with path onto Farrell Street
38.1	Cross Farrell Street with path then right; turn left at corner
38.4	Cross US 7 at light to Home Avenue
38.9	Cross RR tracks to Austin Drive
39.4	Right on path
39.6	Straight on road bordered by boulders
39.9	Bear left on path-road curves right
40.2	Right on Harrison Avenue when path ends
40.4	Left on path just before tracks
41.6	King Street ferry landing

50-mile ride

20.9	Right on NY 22 south (sign after turn)
21.9	Left with NY 22
24.7	Left on Whallons Bay Road in Whallonsburg
24.9	Bear left under railroad overpass
25.6	Left with Whallons Bay Road at intersection
26.3	Right with Whallons Bay Road at Middle Road
27.6	Left on Lake Shore Road at lakefront
30.3+	Right into Essex ferry landing
	This is mile 21.8 above; add 8.5 miles to remaining cues.

Lake Champlain

NEW YORK

VERMONT

Ausable Chasm

PORT KENT

Ferry

Soper Rd.

KEESEVILLE

Mace Chasm Rd.

Highlands Rd.

Willsboro Bay

Long Pond

WILLSBORO

Octagonal Stone Schoolhouse

Boquet River

WHALLONSBURG

ESSEX

Ferry

360° Panorama

START
BURLINGTON

SOUTH BURLINGTON

Spear St.

SHELBURNE

Shelburne Museum

SHELBURNE FALLS

Greenbush Rd.

Lake Rd.

CHARLOTTE

8. BURLINGTON–ESSEX

| 0 | | 2 | | 4 mi |
| 0 | 2 | | 4 km | |

N

© The Countryman Press

more interesting place to do so than Port Kent, which offers little more than a small restaurant. Lastly, the 50-mile option provides some great cycling and views. Those riding it clockwise will generally use the LCB route of Highlands Road and Essex County 28, leaving NY 22 just past Long Pond.

The cues start at the Port Kent ferry landing in NY State, assuming that you have taken the ferry over from Burlington.

Board the ferry at King Street in Burlington.

0.0 Ride uphill on NY 373 west in Port Kent.

1.8 Bear left on Soper Road/Essex 17.

2.8 Turn left on Mace Chasm Road—this will become rolling in a mile and remain so to US 9.

4.4 Cross Port Douglas road at a stop sign.

7.3 Turn left on US 9 south at a T-intersection.

8.5 Turn left on NY 22 south at the light—be ready to climb for the next mile and a half.

10.0 Top of the climb—the next 6.5 miles are gloriously downhill.

15.0 Camel's Hump is visible straight ahead.

16.7 Turn left with NY 22 as it crosses the Boquet River in Willsboro.

16.8 Turn right with NY 22—the Willsboro Historic Museum is located here.

17.4 Turn left with NY 22 where Essex 66/Middle Road is on the right.
For 50-mile ride: *Turn right on Essex 66/Middle Road here and continue at the cues below.*

21.8 Turn left into the Essex ferry landing.
This ferry generally runs every half hour and Essex is a great town to explore if you have the time.

21.9 Ride on VT F5 from the Charlotte ferry landing.

22.3 Turn right on VT F5.

23.3 Turn left on Lake Road.

25.1 Ride through a single lane covered bridge (second shortest in Vermont) with lake views and a park just past it with picnic tables, restrooms and swimming—there may be a day-use fee.

26.6 Turn left on Greenbush Road at a T-intersection.

28.3 Turn right on Bostwick Road where Beach Road is straight.

30.2 Turn left on US 7 north—this will have moderate to heavy traffic, but you're only on it for just over a mile and it's mostly downhill. The Shelburne Museum in on the left.

31.5 Turn right on Webster Road just after the bridge.

31.6 Bear right on Webster Road (no sign).

32.7 Turn left on Spear Street at the three-way stop.

35.6 Overlook Park is on the left—great views, especially late in the day.

36.4 Turn left on the bike path at a white barn just before Swift Street.

36.9 Make a very sharp downhill right turn with the bike path, after which you cross a wooden bridge, which can be dangerous when wet.

37.7 Turn right with the wider path at the bottom of the downhill.

37.8 Turn left on Swift Street with the bike path.

37.8+ Turn right with the path onto Farrell Street.

38.1 Cross Farrell Street with the path and turn right, then left at the corner.

38.4 Cross US 7 at the light to Home Avenue.

38.9 Cross the RR tracks to Austin Drive.

39.4 Turn right on the bike path.

39.6 Ride straight on the road bordered by boulders.
There is a side path to a rocky beach on the left, with pavilions and restrooms nearby.

An avenue of trees framing Camel's Hump on Whallons Bay Road

39.9 Bear left on the bike path where the road curves right.

40.2 Turn right on Harrison Avenue when the bike path ends.

40.4 Turn left on the bike path just before the tracks.

41.3 Note the carved white boulders along the shore at a small peninsular park.

41.6 King Street ferry landing—end of tour.

50-MILE RIDE

20.9 Turn right on NY 22 south (sign after turn).

21.9 Octagonal stone schoolhouse on left in Boquet.

21.9+ Turn left with NY 22.

24.7 Turn left on Whallons Bay Road in Whallonsburg.

24.9 Bear left under the railroad overpass.

25.6 Turn left with Whallons Bay Road at the intersection.

25.8 There is a great 360-degree panorama from this location.

26.3 Bear right with Whallons Bay Road at Middle Road.

26.7 An avenue of trees on the downhill frames Camel's Hump.

27.6 Turn left on Lake Shore Road at the lakefront.

30.3 Straight at the flasher in Essex.

30.3+ Turn right into the Essex ferry landing.
This is mile 21.8; add 8.5 miles to the remaining cues.

ST. ALBANS AND THE VERMONT NORTHERN AND QUEBEC TOURS

Two curious residents of the extensive farming area surrounding St. Albans

ALTHOUGH THE FIRST EDITION of this book doesn't have any tours originating in St. Albans, it is the largest community on the Vermont side of the lake north of Burlington and thereby qualifies as the regional center. St. Albans has a long history as a railroad town and is currently the headquarters of the New England Central Railroad, as well as the northern terminus of Amtrak's "Vermonter." Its major claim to fame is as the site of the northernmost action of the Civil War, achieved when 22 Confederate soldiers in civilian clothes entered the town from Canada on October 19, 1864. They held up three banks and escaped back to Canada with just over $200,000. Although the group was captured in Montreal and tried, they were never extradited despite Lincoln's attempts, and they later returned to the south to fight for the Confederacy.

In 1866 St. Albans was again involved in another international incident, when a guerrilla force of several hundred (other estimates are into the thousands) Fenians arrived on special trains from Boston, determined to liberate Canada from the British and establish an Irish Free State. They camped on the town green and then headed across the border, but the Canadians declared martial law and the Fenians retreated after reaching Frelighsburg, Quebec. President Johnson intervened and the group was met by U.S. troops upon their return to St. Albans, and soon sent back to Boston under armed escort.

St. Albans has a healthy downtown business area and seems re-energized, no doubt assisted by the ever-expanding suburban sprawl created by Burlington's growth. The town green is a pleasant place to relax or enjoy an alfresco lunch, perhaps purchased from the nearby Jeff's Maine Seafood. The Franklin County Historical Society fronts the green and is open from 1–4 PM, June–September. Swanton is the other major town in the region, although much smaller than St. Albans. It also has a large green in the middle of its small commercial center.

For those with hybrid or mountain bikes, you might consider a ride on the Missisquoi Valley Rail Trail, which begins in St. Albans on an abandoned rail bed and extends for almost 27 miles to Richford. The trail is composed of fine stone, although some sections are of coarser gravel. Snowmobiles are allowed in winter, but no motorized vehicles can use the trail during cycling season.

The area of Quebec directly north of the lake is unrelentingly flat farmland, but as you move east to the eastern townships things become a bit more rolling. This region is very popular for cycling and draws riders from Montreal, Quebec City, and other urban centers. There are several long-distance rail trails (dirt/gravel) here and the Velo Quebec organization is working to develop additional cycling routes and resources, much as Lake Champlain Bikeways is doing around the lake.

Tourism Info

The St. Albans Area Chamber of Commerce, 2 North Main Street (802-524-2444 or www.stalbanschamber.com)

The Swanton Chamber of Commerce (802-868-7200) maintains a small information booth near the green.

Bike Shops

St. Albans—North Star Cyclery, 16 S. Main Street (802-524-2049)

Swanton—Porter's Bike shop, 116 Grand Avenue (802-868-7417)

Bedford—Velo Evasion, 797 Rte 202 (450-248-7188)

Bedford—Velofix (see tour 11)

9

Milton–St. Albans

*Back roads, dairy farms,
and the lake*

- ■ **DISTANCE**: 32, 42, and 50 miles.

- ■ **TERRAIN/DIFFICULTY**: Generally flat to lightly rolling with 2 miles moderately rolling; moderate.

- ■ **START**: Public Works parking along Ice House Road off VT 7, near the dam just north of Milton.

- ■ **GETTING THERE/PARKING**: I-89 to Exit 17 then left at the top of the ramp for US 7 north. Turn left/north on US 7 and follow it through the town of Milton. Ice House Road is just after Main Street on the right.

These loops were among the earliest that I scouted and rode in the region. They looked attractive on the map since it seemed there was a "ladder" structure with parallel north and south routes, while riders could decide which "rung" to take across to the lake based on their riding preferences, the weather, and how they were feeling that day. In the "old days" we simply rode north on US 7 from Milton to St. Albans, but for this book I've found a much more pleasant and scenic, not to mention less traffic-intensive, route using back roads for the ride north. There's a little climbing shortly after leaving Milton and some more toward the end of the ride, but in between it is largely flat or lightly rolling. The loop you choose will determine how much time you spend riding along the lake.

The town of Milton was chartered in 1763 by Governor Wentworth of New Hampshire, but was not settled until 1782. West Milton, on the banks of the Lamoille River, was the first part of the town to be settled. (An interesting bit of trivia on this river's name: apparently Champlain marked his map at this point with *"la mouette"* for seagull,

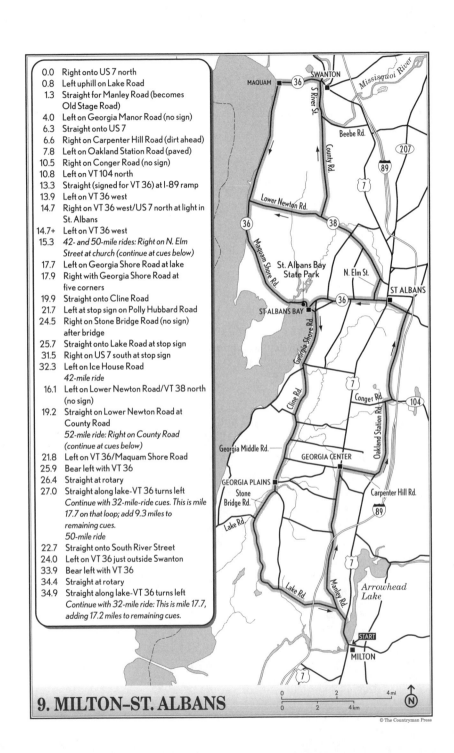

0.0	Right onto US 7 north
0.8	Left uphill on Lake Road
1.3	Straight for Manley Road (becomes Old Stage Road)
4.0	Left on Georgia Manor Road (no sign)
6.3	Straight onto US 7
6.6	Right on Carpenter Hill Road (dirt ahead)
7.8	Left on Oakland Station Road (paved)
10.5	Right on Conger Road (no sign)
10.8	Left on VT 104 north
13.3	Straight (signed for VT 36) at I-89 ramp
13.9	Left on VT 36 west
14.7	Right on VT 36 west/US 7 north at light in St. Albans
14.7+	Left on VT 36 west
15.3	*42- and 50-mile rides: Right on N. Elm Street at church (continue at cues below)*
17.7	Left on Georgia Shore Road at lake
17.9	Right with Georgia Shore Road at five corners
19.9	Straight onto Cline Road
21.7	Left at stop sign on Polly Hubbard Road
24.5	Right on Stone Bridge Road (no sign) after bridge
25.7	Straight onto Lake Road at stop sign
31.5	Right on US 7 south at stop sign
32.3	Left on Ice House Road *42-mile ride*
16.1	Left on Lower Newton Road/VT 38 north (no sign)
19.2	Straight on Lower Newton Road at County Road *52-mile ride: Right on County Road (continue at cues below)*
21.8	Left on VT 36/Maquam Shore Road
25.9	Bear left with VT 36
26.4	Straight at rotary
27.0	Straight along lake-VT 36 turns left *Continue with 32-mile-ride cues. This is mile 17.7 on that loop; add 9.3 miles to remaining cues.* *50-mile ride*
22.7	Straight onto South River Street
24.0	Left on VT 36 just outside Swanton
33.9	Bear left with VT 36
34.4	Straight at rotary
34.9	Straight along lake-VT 36 turns left *Continue with 32-mile ride: This is mile 17.7, adding 17.2 miles to remaining cues.*

9. MILTON–ST. ALBANS

© The Countryman Press

but a later cartographer forgot to cross his t's.) The abundant timber in the area provided most of the early income, as schooners could sail up the river to town with the spring high water and load lumber, pulp-wood, and cordwood for Montreal and foreign markets. The seven waterfalls in town provided a valuable resource to power sawmills, gristmills, and various other manufacturing industries. The production of potash for European markets was another lucrative early industry, but dairying and farming eventually became the mainstays of the town's economy.

Fifteen miles of riding on country roads brings you to St. Albans, the largest town in western Vermont north of Burlington. If you're ready for lunch, you will find many options here. This is also where the shortest loop heads west to the lake and then south back to the start. The two longer rides continue northwest from St. Albans, with the longest loop continuing north to Swanton, another possible lunch stop. More riding near the lake follows, before the route turns inland through dairy country to the town of Georgia Plains. The terrain becomes more sharply rolling for a few miles shortly after this, but then you drop back to US 7 and a sweet finish along Arrowhead Lake.

0.0 Turn right onto US 7 north.

Arrowhead Mountain Lake is on the right and Arrowhead Mountain is briefly in view on the left.

0.8 Turn left uphill on Lake Road.

1.3 Stay straight for Manley Road (becomes Old Stage Road).

4.0 Turn left on Georgia Manor Road (no sign) at a T-intersection.

5.3 There is an interesting wood pattern on a pair of barns to the left, both over a century old.

6.3 Ride straight onto US 7 with caution!

6.6 Turn right on Carpenter Hill Road.

7.0 The surface changes to dirt on a downhill—it is smooth hardpack, but watch for potholes.

7.8 Turn left on Oakland Station Road (paved) at a T-intersection—the next few miles provide delightful, quiet riding.

10.5 Turn right on Conger Road (no sign) at a T-intersection.

10.8 Turn left on VT 104 north.

13.3 Stay straight (signed for VT 36) at I-89.

13.9 Turn left on VT 36 west.

14.7 Turn right on VT 36 west/US 7 north at the light in St. Albans with the town green on your right.
If you want an early lunch, I recommend Jeff's Maine Seafood at the far end of the green, although there are other options in town.

14.7+ Turn left on VT 36 west.

14.9 The New England Central Railroad headquarters is on the right. Formerly, a large and handsome passenger train shed stood at this location.

15.3 *For 42 and 50- mile rides:* Turn right on N. Elm Street just before a brick church and continue at the cues below.

17.7 Turn left on Georgia Shore Road at the lake.

17.9 Turn right with Georgia Shore Road at five corners.

19.9 Ride straight onto Cline Road.

21.7 Turn left at the stop sign on Polly Hubbard Road, which becomes Georgia Middle Road at the next intersection.

24.5 Turn right on Stone Bridge Road (no sign) just after crossing the bridge in Georgia Plains.

25.7 Continue straight at a stop sign onto Lake Road, where it joins from the right—you'll have rolling terrain for the next 2 miles.

28.4 There are ruins of a small country sawmill on the left.

29.7 A small "Breadloaf" style barn is on the left.

31.5 Turn right on US 7 south at the bottom of the hill.

32.3 Turn left on Ice House Road—end of the tour.

Evening rush hour near Georgia Plains

If you want some post-ride refreshment, the appropriately named Finish Line Pub is on US 7 just around the corner from Ice House Road.

42-MILE RIDE

15.7 Cross RR tracks—the NECR yard is left with the engine facility to the right.

16.1 Turn left on Lower Newton Road/VT 38 north (no sign) at a T-intersection.

17.6 Brake for a railroad track on a downhill.

17.9 Cross Kellogg Road.

19.2 Stay straight on Lower Newton Road at County Road.
For 52-mile ride: *Turn right on County Road and continue at the cues below.*

21.8 Turn left on VT 36/Maquam Shore Road as you reach the lake.

25.9 Bear left with VT 36 just past an ancient gas station with two generations of pumps being slowly swallowed by tall grass.
Option: *Turn right here for additional lakeshore riding to Hathaway Point. It's about 3 miles to Kill Kare State Park (admission fee) at the end of the peninsula.*

26.4 Straight at the rotary.

26.5 St. Albans Bay town park is on the right—this is a good lunch spot with restrooms in the main building, which should be open even if this gate is closed.

27.0 Straight along the lake where VT 36 turns left. There are stores here.
Continue with the 32-mile-ride cues. This is mile 17.7 on that loop, so add 9.3 miles to the remaining cues.

50-MILE RIDE

22.7 Caution—cross RR track at an angle and then ride straight onto South River Street.

You're riding with the Missisquoi River to your right as you approach Swanton.

23.7 The Swanton railroad station restoration is on the left.
The handsome 1875 structure has been lovingly restored and the museum is open 11–3 PM, Tuesday through Saturday. Behind the station is an old turntable pit and the stone stalls from the roundhouse. The stone bridge piers from the former line that ran here can be seen in the river.

24.0 Turn left on VT 36 just outside Swanton.
Turn right on VT 78 east just ahead for food or supplies in town.

25.5 You are forced left as VT 36 reaches the lake—Swanton Beach park is here.

29.8 Stay straight where Lower Newton Road is left.
Note: See 42-mile ride for more info on the next few cues.

33.9 Bear left with VT 36.

34.4 Straight at the rotary.

34.5 St. Albans Bay town park is on the right.

34.9 Straight along the lake where VT 36 turns left.
Continue with the 32-mile-ride cues. This is mile 17.7 on that loop, so add 17.2 miles to the remaining cues.

10

Swanton–Philipsburg

A "taste" of Quebec

- **DISTANCE:** 36 or 59 miles.

- **TERRAIN/DIFFICULTY:** Generally lightly rolling with 3 miles moderately rolling; somewhat more rolling on the long ride; moderate for the short and moderately difficult on the long.

- **START:** Swanton Green—corner of Canada Street/US 7 and Grand Avenue.

- **GETTING THERE/PARKING:** I-89 to Exit 21 and then about a mile west to Swanton. Plenty of parking in town.

This tour offers generally easy riding with good scenery and lightly traveled roads. Although there isn't much riding near the lake, you do pedal next to it in the lovely Quebec village of Philipsburg, which is the recommended lunch stop on the short ride. The longer loop initially heads east after crossing into Canada and passes through the equally charming town of Frelighsburg, where you're likely to see lots of cyclists, particularly on summer weekends.

The riding on both loops is flat and lightly rolling to the border. The short ride then has rolling terrain to Philipsburg, but absolutely flat roads from the border back to the start. The long tour goes through an agricultural area in Quebec with orchards and vineyards, which may be open for wine tasting.

Note: I don't recommend doing this tour on the last day of a three-day summer weekend, as the border crossing can be slow due to the amount of traffic returning to the United States from the Montreal area.

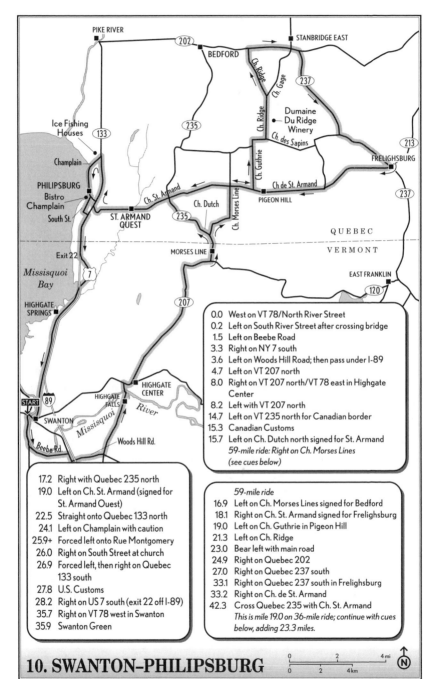

0.0	West on VT 78/North River Street
0.2	Left on South River Street after crossing bridge
1.5	Left on Beebe Road
3.3	Right on NY 7 south
3.6	Left on Woods Hill Road; then pass under I-89
4.7	Left on VT 207 north
8.0	Right on VT 207 north/VT 78 east in Highgate Center
8.2	Left with VT 207 north
14.7	Left on VT 235 north for Canadian border
15.3	Canadian Customs
15.7	Left on Ch. Dutch north signed for St. Armand
	59-mile ride: Right on Ch. Morses Lines (see cues below)

17.2	Right with Quebec 235 north
19.0	Left on Ch. St. Armand (signed for St. Armand Ouest)
22.5	Straight onto Quebec 133 north
24.1	Left on Champlain with caution
25.9+	Forced left onto Rue Montgomery
26.0	Right on South Street at church
26.9	Forced left, then right on Quebec 133 south
27.8	U.S. Customs
28.2	Right on US 7 south (exit 22 off I-89)
35.7	Right on VT 78 west in Swanton
35.9	Swanton Green

	59-mile ride
16.9	Left on Ch. Morses Lines signed for Bedford
18.1	Right on Ch. St. Armand signed for Frelighsburg
19.0	Left on Ch. Guthrie in Pigeon Hill
21.3	Left on Ch. Ridge
23.0	Bear left with main road
24.9	Right on Quebec 202
27.0	Right on Quebec 237 south
33.1	Right on Quebec 237 south in Frelighsburg
33.2	Right on Ch. de St. Armand
42.3	Cross Quebec 235 with Ch. St. Armand
	This is mile 19.0 on 36-mile ride; continue with cues below, adding 23.3 miles.

10. SWANTON–PHILIPSBURG

0		2		4 mi
0		2	4 km	

N

0.0 Ride west on VT 78/North River Street.

0.2 Turn left on South River Street after crossing the Missisquoi River.

0.6 The Swanton railroad station restoration is on the right.
The handsome 1875 structure has been lovingly restored and the museum is open 11–3, Tuesday to Saturday. Behind the station is an old turntable pit and the stone stalls from the roundhouse. The stone bridge piers from the track that formerly ran here can be seen in the river.

1.5 Turn left on Beebe Road.
This is some mellow riding with the river on the left and cornfields on the right.

3.3 Turn right on VT 7 south at a T-intersection.

3.6 Turn left on Woods Hill Road and pass under I-89.

4.7 Turn left on VT 207 north.

7.5 The handsome Highgate Manor Inn is on the left entering Highgate Falls.

8.0 Turn right on VT 207 north/VT 78 east in Highgate Center.

8.1 There is a small park with benches on the right and stores nearby if you want a break.

8.2 Turn left with VT 207 north.

14.1 The distant notched mountain ahead is Jay Peak.

14.7 Turn left on VT 235 north for the Canadian border.

15.3 Canadian Customs at Morses Line border station.

15.7 Turn left on Ch. Dutch north signed for St. Armand.
For 59-mile ride: *Turn right on Ch. Morses Lines here and continue at cues below.*

17.2 Turn right at a T-intersection with Quebec 235 north.

19.0 Turn left on Ch. St. Armand (signed for St. Armand Ouest).
You will have rolling hills for the next 3 miles. There are sometimes blind turns, so stay right and watch for approaching traffic.

20.6 St. Armand Ouest—there is a general store here.

22.5 Ride straight onto Quebec 133 north, which is a divided highway with lane-wide shoulders and generally light traffic.
You may well wonder why you're riding on such a road, but you will soon be amply rewarded.

24.1 Turn left on Champlain with caution!
Experienced riders can look, signal and ride to the left turn lane when there is no traffic. Others may prefer to stop in the shoulder and walk across when it's clear.

24.5 You can see ice-fishing houses in summer storage on the right.

24.8 Lake Champlain—this is Missisquoi Bay, the far northeastern corner of the lake.

25.2 Enter Philipsburg, an attractive small village.

25.8 Public picnic tables and benches by the lake—please respect signed private areas along the lake. Across the street is a 1784 log cabin.

25.9 Bistro Champlain is on the right—open for lunch and dinner on Friday, Saturday, and Sunday. Good food is available at a reasonable price.

25.9+ Forced left onto Rue Montgomery.

26.0 Turn right on South Street at the brick church.

26.9 After forced left, turn right on Quebec 133 south.

27.8 US Customs at the Border station.

28.2 Turn right on US 7 south (exit 22 off I-89).

35.7 Turn right on VT 78 west in Swanton.

35.9 Swanton Green—end of the tour.

59-MILE RIDE

16.9 Turn left on Ch. Morses Lines signed for Bedford.

18.1 Turn right on Ch. St. Armand signed for Frelighsburg.

Ice-fishing houses in summer storage in Philipsburg

19.0 Turn left on Ch. Guthrie in Pigeon Hill.

19.1 There is a giant's walking stick leaning against a shed on the left—or is it a shepherd's crook?

19.2 There is an implausible canoe in a miniscule pond on the left.

21.3 Turn left on Ch. Ridge.

21.6 The Dumaine Du Ridge winery is on the right and likely open for tasting.

23.0 Bear left with the main road.

24.9 Turn right on Quebec 202 at a T-intersection—there can be moderate traffic on this road.

26.6 Gladacres farm is on the left.

The prevalence of English names in this region is largely due to it being originally populated by Tories/Loyalists as the American Revolution broke out, and continuing through and after the war.

27.0 Turn right on Quebec 237 south—this road is lightly to moderately rolling.

33.0 There is a folksy mural on the right entering Frelighsburg.

33.1 Turn right on Quebec 237 south in Frelighsburg.

The recommended lunch stop is Aux 2 Clochers restaurant straight ahead—try to sit on the deck over the river, but beware of smokers. Another option is the patisserie/crêperie on the right just after the turn. If you have your own food or just want a rest in the shade, there are benches and picnic tables in front of the town hall at this intersection.

33.2 Turn right on Ch. de St Armand where Quebec 237 turns sharply left.

Hopefully you didn't eat too much for lunch as you have a half-mile climb leaving town.

38.2 Continue straight at the crossroads in Pigeon Hill.

39.8 Ride straight where Ch. Morses Line is on the left.

42.3 Cross Quebec 235 with Ch. St Armand—you'll have rolling hills for the next 3 miles.

This is mile 19.0 on the 36-mile ride—continue with those cues and add 23.3 miles to them.

Bedford–Philipsburg

Route de Vin

- **DISTANCE:** 25 or 41 miles
- **TERRAIN/DIFFICULTY:** Generally lightly rolling with some moderately rolling; easy to moderate.
- **START:** Corner of Rue Principal and Quebec Route 235 in Bedford, Eastern Townships, Quebec.
- **GETTING THERE/PARKING:** I-89/Quebec 133 to Pike River, then Quebec Route 202 east to Bedford. Free parking in town center.

This is the only tour in the book that starts in Quebec, although it covers some of the same territory as tour 10, in particular the lovely village of Philipsburg. Both loops leave the lively small town of Bedford on a road signed for Route de Vin, and a winery is indeed passed 6 miles into the ride. The short ride encounters a few miles of rolling terrain as it heads west for Philipsburg shortly after this, while the long tour continues south and crosses the border into Vermont. After passing through Highgate Center, this route turns northwest toward the lake and crosses back into Canada at Philipsburg. The return to Bedford is virtually flat, much of it through open fields in farming country. Near the end of the tour you pass through the pleasant and green village of Mystic, which almost seems an oasis after the long stretches of cropland.

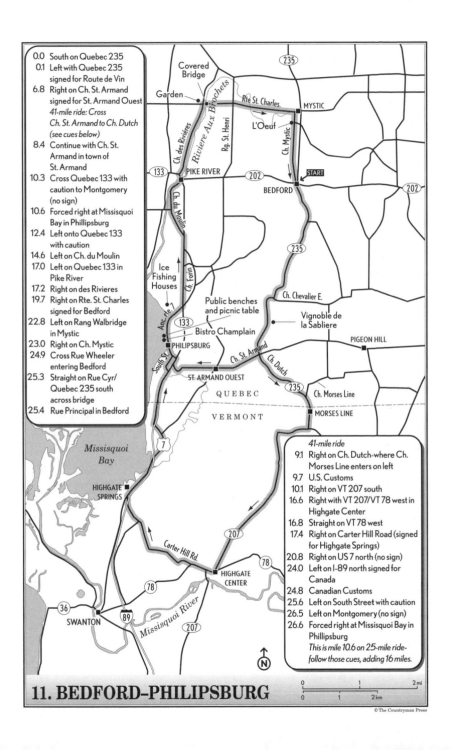

0.0	South on Quebec 235
0.1	Left with Quebec 235 signed for Route de Vin
6.8	Right on Ch. St. Armand signed for St. Armand Ouest
	41-mile ride: Cross Ch. St. Armand to Ch. Dutch (see cues below)
8.4	Continue with Ch. St. Armand in town of St. Armand
10.3	Cross Quebec 133 with caution to Montgomery (no sign)
10.6	Forced right at Missisquoi Bay in Phillipsburg
12.4	Left onto Quebec 133 with caution
14.6	Left on Ch. du Moulin
17.0	Left on Quebec 133 in Pike River
17.2	Right on des Rivieres
19.7	Right on Rte. St. Charles signed for Bedford
22.8	Left on Rang Walbridge in Mystic
23.0	Right on Ch. Mystic
24.9	Cross Rue Wheeler entering Bedford
25.3	Straight on Rue Cyr/ Quebec 235 south across bridge
25.4	Rue Principal in Bedford

Covered Bridge
Garden
Rivière Aux Brochets
Rte St. Charles
MYSTIC
L'Oeuf
Ch. Mystic
Ch. des Rivières
Rg. St. Henri
Ch. du Moulin
PIKE RIVER
133
202
START
BEDFORD
202
235
Ch. Forin
Ice Fishing Houses
Anc. rte.
Ch. Chevalier E.
Public benches and picnic table
Vignoble de la Sabliere
PIGEON HILL
Bistro Champlain
133
PHILIPSBURG
South St.
Ch. St. Armand
Ch. Dutch
ST. ARMAND OUEST
235
Ch. Morses Line
QUEBEC
VERMONT
MORSES LINE
Missisquoi Bay
7
HIGHGATE SPRINGS
207
Carter Hill Rd.
78
HIGHGATE CENTER
78
36
89
SWANTON
Missisquoi River
207

	41-mile ride
9.1	Right on Ch. Dutch-where Ch. Morses Line enters on left
9.7	U.S. Customs
10.1	Right on VT 207 south
16.6	Right with VT 207/VT 78 west in Highgate Center
16.8	Straight on VT 78 west
17.4	Right on Carter Hill Road (signed for Highgate Springs)
20.8	Right on US 7 north (no sign)
24.0	Left on I-89 north signed for Canada
24.8	Canadian Customs
25.6	Left on South Street with caution
26.5	Left on Montgomery (no sign)
26.6	Forced right at Missisquoi Bay in Phillipsburg
	This is mile 10.6 on 25-mile ride- follow those cues, adding 16 miles.

N

11. BEDFORD–PHILIPSBURG

| 0 | | 1 | | 2 mi |
| 0 | 1 | | 2 km | |

0.0 Ride south on Quebec 235.

0.1 Turn left with Quebec 235 signed for Route de Vin.

4.5 Follow Quebec 235 at a zigzag where Ch. Chevalier crosses.

6.1 Vignoble de la Sabliere is on the left, which may be open for tastings.

6.8 Turn right on Ch. St. Armand signed for St. Armand Ouest.
For 41-mile ride: *Cross Ch. St. Armand to Ch. Dutch and continue at the cues below.*

8.4 Continue with Ch. St. Armand in the town of St. Armand. There is a general store here.
The next 2 miles are quite rolling with some blind turns.

10.3 Cross Quebec 133 with caution to Montgomery (no sign).

10.6 You are forced right at Missisquoi Bay in the small village of Philipsburg.
On the water side at the turn is Bistro Champlain, which is open for lunch and dinner on Friday, Saturday, and Sunday.

10.7 Public picnic tables and benches along the lake—please respect signed private areas.
Across the street is a 1784 log cabin.

11.9 On the left you can see ice-fishing shacks in summer storage.

12.4 Turn left with caution onto Quebec 133.
There is a good shoulder here, although the traffic is high speed. An alternative for those who don't mind dirt is to take Ch. du Moulin (directly across) instead, which then recrosses 133 just as you turn off it, although your mileage will be a few tenths of a mile higher.

14.6 Turn left on Ch. du Moulin—there is a left turn lane here, or you can wait on the shoulder until it is safe to cross.

17.0 Turn left on Quebec 133 in Pike River.

17.2 Turn right on des Rivieres at the depanneur.

19.7 Turn right on Route St. Charles signed for Bedford.

Round barn with gables near Mystic, Quebec

The house across from this turn has an excellent garden and welcomes visitors, but Suzy the dog will probably bark at you anyway.

19.8 Pass through a covered bridge over the Riviere aux Brochets.

22.8 Turn left on Rang Walbridge at a T-intersection in the village of Mystic, which seems almost shockingly green and lush after the miles of riding through open fields.

23.0 Turn right on Ch. Mystic.
At this turn is the L'Oeuf Restaurant, Auberge and Chocolatier.

23.1 On the right is a quite unusual round barn with gables.

24.3 There is a sign for Velofix at a house on the right.
One assumes they do bicycle repairs, but it looks like a part-time operation.

24.9 Cross Rue Wheeler entering Bedford.

25.3 Ride straight on Rue Cyr/Quebec 235 south across the bridge.

25.4 Rue Principal in Bedford—end of the tour.

41-MILE RIDE

6.8 The next 2 miles are more rolling in very pleasant countryside.

9.1 Bear right on Ch. Dutch where Ch. Morses Line enters on the left.

9.7 Stop at U.S. Customs.

10.1 Turn right on VT 207 south at a T-intersection.

16.6 Turn right with VT 207/VT 78 west in Highgate Center.

16.7 There is a small park with benches on the left, and general stores nearby.

16.8 Continue straight on VT 78 west.

17.4 Bear right on Carter Hill Road signed for Highgate Springs.

20.8 Turn right on US 7 north (no sign) after crossing over I-89 and shortly enter Highgate Springs, where there is a general store.

24.0 Turn left on I-89 north signed for Canada.

24.8 Canadian Customs.

25.6 Turn left on South Street at the bottom of a hill.
There is a left-turn lane here, but you may prefer to stop and wait on the shoulder until it is safe to cross.

26.5 Turn left on Montgomery (no sign) at a T-intersection.

26.6 Forced right at Missisquoi Bay in the small village of Philipsburg.
This is mile 10.6 on the 25-mile ride and you should follow those cues from here, adding 16 miles to them.

THE LAKE CHAMPLAIN ISLANDS TOURS

Prancing-horse barn doors on VT 225 just south of the Canadian border

MY OLDEST MEMORY of the Lake Champlain region is of the Lake Champlain Islands. I had been at Expo '67 in Montreal in the fall of that year with my dad, and we drove down the islands on our return trip to New Jersey. I can imagine my father looking at a map before leaving Montreal, noting that US 2 snakes its way down the middle of the lake through a series of islands and thinking it would be a nice break from the interstate. It was a rainy day, but that didn't stop us from enjoying our drive and I recall thinking that I would like to come back to this region. When I finally returned almost two decades later to Lake Champlain it was in the same area, riding the loop that is tour 14 in this book.

Samuel de Champlain first saw the lake he modestly named after himself in 1609, when he joined a party of Canadian Algonquins on a raid against the Iroquois nation. In 1666 a French fort was built to defend the area against Indians by a company commanded by Captain Pierre de St. Paul, Sieur de la Motte. Jesuit priests, who were garrisoned with the troops, built a shrine here dedicated to St. Anne. The garrison was called back to Canada after only four years and the fort destroyed, but the la Motte name stayed on. In the late 1800s a new shrine to St. Anne was built here and is today one of the main draws for visitors to the islands.

The Vermont Legislature bestowed grants for the islands to Ethan and Ira Allen and a few other Green Mountain Boys in 1779. The grant was for land originally called "Two Heroes," named after the brothers (some sources say they were actually named by the immodest brothers themselves, who were perhaps following in Champlain's footsteps), but was split into North and South Hero in 1788. Grand Isle, first known

as Middle Hero, was split off from South Hero in 1798. Alburg, formerly called Allenburgh, was granted in 1781 to Ira Allen and a large
group of Revolutionary War veterans. Enos Wood, Ebenezer Allen, and
Alexander Gordon (of Gordon Landing) were the first to actually home-
stead on the islands in 1873.

You can visit a survivor of the early history of the islands in Grand
Isle. The Hyde Log Cabin was constructed around 1783 by Jedediah
Hyde Jr., who had come to the islands with his father to do surveying
work. The cabin, which has been moved a couple of miles from its original location, was lived in by many generations of the Hyde family for
almost 150 years and is claimed to be the oldest surviving log cabin in
the country.

There are several motels on the islands as well as inns and B&Bs.
There are only a few opportunities for anything approaching formal
dining, but casual food is more widely available. The Royal Lipizzan
Stallions make their summer home on North Hero and give performances from mid-July to late August.

Tourism Info

Lake Champlain Islands Chamber of Commerce, US 2, North Hero (www.champlainis-
lands.com/chamber/)

A site with some interesting history and old photographs of US 2 through the islands:
(http://www.letmeshowyouvermont.com/2-1.htm)

Bike Shops

There are no bike shops on the Lake Champlain Islands and the nearest ones are in Burlington, Swanton, and Plattsburgh. So make certain
that your bike is in good condition before starting any of the rides in
this region. There is a small bike-rental location a bit south of the
shrine on Isle La Motte and he may be willing to do basic repairs in an
emergency.

12

South Hero–Grand Isle

Log cabins, tiny castles,
split-rail fences, and sublime views

- **DISTANCE:** 26 or 32 miles.

- **TERRAIN/DIFFICULTY:** Generally flat to lightly rolling; easy.

- **START:** South Hero at intersection of US 2 and South Street.

- **GETTING THERE/PARKING:** Exit 17 from I-89 signed for the Lake Champlain Islands and the ferry to NY state. Drive on US 2 N for 8.5 miles to South Hero. The owner of Seb's French Fries doesn't mind cyclists parking there for a limited time, but please park in back and check with them first if they're open. There's a port-a-potty out back, largely hidden by a pine tree. You can also park at the South Hero town offices, just west on US 2, on weekends.

M ile for mile, this tour is more scenically rich than any other ride described here. This is the only tour with a substantial amount of dirt roads, sometimes with a rough surface. However, the amazing beauty of this ride would make it criminal to omit it from the book. There are many lake views, some with distant vistas and others offering intimate bays. For those riders whose tires never touch dirt, I suggest tour 14 instead. However, road bikes with a tire size of at least 28 mm should be OK—so long as you don't have your tires overly inflated. This would be an excellent ride for families with children who can handle the distance—either riding their own bikes, being towed or carried.

One of the visual riches of this ride is an amazing variety of well-aged, wooden structures—including log cabins, houses, barns, and other farm buildings. Many if not most of the farms are no longer working, but I am impressed with how well most of these older structures are maintained. Few are painted, instead left to weather naturally and show their grain. There is also a greater concentration of

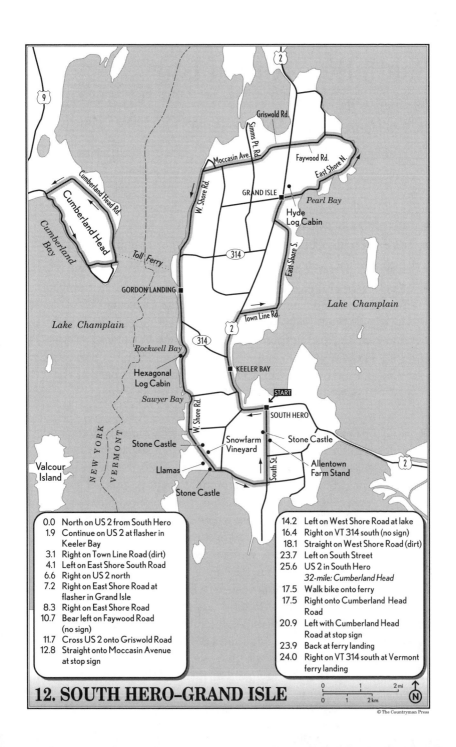

2	
9	

Griswold Rd.

Simms Pt. Rd.

Moccasin Ave.

Faywood Rd.

East Shore N.

Cumberland Head Rd.

Cumberland Head

W. Shore Rd.

GRAND ISLE

Pearl Bay

Hyde
Log Cabin

Cumberland Bay

Toll Ferry

314

East Shore S.

Lake Champlain

GORDON LANDING

Lake Champlain

Town Line Rd.

314

2

Rockwell Bay

Hexagonal
Log Cabin

KEELER BAY

Sawyer Bay

W. Shore Rd.

START

SOUTH HERO

Snowfarm
Vineyard

Stone Castle

Stone Castle

Allentown
Farm Stand

South St.

Llamas

2

Valcour
Island

NEW YORK

VERMONT

Stone Castle

0.0	North on US 2 from South Hero
1.9	Continue on US 2 at flasher in Keeler Bay
3.1	Right on Town Line Road (dirt)
4.1	Left on East Shore South Road
6.6	Right on US 2 north
7.2	Right on East Shore Road at flasher in Grand Isle
8.3	Right on East Shore Road
10.7	Bear left on Faywood Road (no sign)
11.7	Cross US 2 onto Griswold Road
12.8	Straight onto Moccasin Avenue at stop sign

14.2	Left on West Shore Road at lake
16.4	Right on VT 314 south (no sign)
18.1	Straight on West Shore Road (dirt)
23.7	Left on South Street
25.6	US 2 in South Hero
	32-mile: Cumberland Head
17.5	Walk bike onto ferry
17.5	Right onto Cumberland Head Road
20.9	Left with Cumberland Head Road at stop sign
23.9	Back at ferry landing
24.0	Right on VT 314 south at Vermont ferry landing

12. SOUTH HERO–GRAND ISLE

0	1	2 mi
0	1	2 km

N

© The Countryman Press

split-rail fences than I've ever seen elsewhere; young Abe Lincoln could have made a good living here. Gray foxes are common in this area (I saw two while doing the ride in early May), so keep on the lookout for them.

What really makes this tour special, particularly for children of all ages, is a series of amazingly well crafted miniature castles constructed of very small stones along the route. These were built by Harry Barber, the son of a Swiss stonemason who worked in the area as a farmhand between the early 1920s and late 1950s, and who picked up the stones while doing his daily duties. If you want more information on Barber and his castles, stop at the town office on a weekday and they'll provide copies of some published articles for a donation.

0.0 Ride north on US 2 from South Hero.

Leaving South Hero you have 3 miles on US 2 with some traffic before turning off onto very quiet roads with many lake views and some riding right along the lake. US 2 has a good shoulder here and I've always found the traffic on it very respectful of cyclists.

1.9 Continue on US 2 at the flasher in Keeler Bay.

Caution—the shoulder is grooved at the turn.

3.1 Turn right on Town Line Road (dirt).

3.9 There is a good view of the lake and the northern Green Mountains on a downhill.

4.0 Slow down before you reach the next turn, as there is loose stone there and you will be carrying some speed from the downhill.

4.1 Turn left on East Shore South Road.

4.5 Straight at the stop sign—the road is paved ahead.

6.6 Turn right on US 2 north at a T-intersection.

7.0 The Island Supermarket is on the left if you need refreshment or supplies.

7.2 Turn right on East Shore Road at the flasher in Grand Isle.

Option: *Just ahead on US 2 is Hyde Log Cabin, built in 1783 and claimed to be the oldest surviving log cabin in the country. Open July 4 through Labor Day, Thursday through Monday, 11:00 AM to 5:00 PM (802-828-3051).*

7.8 This is a particularly blissful spot as you ride with Pearl Bay just beyond the road to the right and a marsh on the left—red-wing blackbirds are also very happy to be here.

8.1 The handsome Grand Isle Lake House is on the right, billed as a "Special Events Facility."

8.2 East Shore Road becomes dirt.

8.3 Bear right on East Shore Road.

9.8 There is a small lakeside gazebo with chairs on the right.
Although obviously private, it's not posted, so I suspect the owner doesn't mind cyclists taking a brief break here as long as they leave it as clean as they found it.

10.0 The pavement returns.

10.7 Bear left on Faywood Road (no sign).

11.1 The Round Barn Apartments are on the right in an unusual and handsome structure.

11.7 Cross US 2 onto Griswold Road.

12.2 There is an attractive serpentine, low stone wall on the left.

12.8 Straight onto Moccasin Avenue at the stop sign.

13.8 There is a very old log cabin on the right.

14.2 Turn left on West Shore Road at the lake.

16.4 Turn right on VT 314 south (no sign).

16.8 You should see some shaggy, long-horned bulls on the right.

17.4 On the right is the ferry to NY State—there are restrooms in the snack stand.
For 32-mile ride: *Take the ferry to add a short, scenic loop on Cumberland Head—buy a round-trip ticket if doing this. This option is described with cues at the end of the tour.*

18.1 Straight on West Shore Road, which soon turns to dirt.

18.8 From Rockwell Bay there is a view of Valcour Island, which was the site of a famed Revolutionary naval battle.

One of Harry Barber's small stone castles

18.9 There is a unique hexagonal log cabin to the right.

19.9 You are forced left as you approach Sawyer Bay.

21.7 The first of Harry Barber's stone castles is in the yard on the left, just past the mailbox with 214 on it.

21.9 Snowfarm Vineyard is on your left—they may be open for wine tastings.

22.0 There is a view of Camel's Hump straight ahead.

22.1 There are about a dozen llamas on the right, but they are smaller than those I'm familiar with and have a more alpaca-like appearance.

22.2 There is another stone castle on the right at Crescent Bay Farm B&B.

22+ The road surface becomes more gravel-like for a mile.

23.7 Turn left on South Street at the stop sign—the road is paved again.
Shortly after this turn you will pass through apple orchards on both sides of the road.

24.6 The Allentown Farm Stand is on the right—they claim to have been there since 1876.

24.9 The last stone castle is on the left just past a house here.

25.6 US 2 in South Hero—end of the tour.

CUMBERLAND HEAD OPTION

17.5 Walk your bike onto the ferry when instructed by the crew.

17.5 Bear to the right leaving the NY ferry landing and turn right on Cumberland Head Road.

20.9 Turn left with Cumberland Head Road at the stop sign.
The next 3 miles feature a fair amount of riding along the shore of Cumberland Bay with good views.

23.9 Back at the ferry landing.

24.0 Turn right on VT 314 south at the Vermont ferry landing.
Return to the main route and add 6.6 miles to the following cues.

13

Isle La Motte

*A shrine, very quiet roads,
and equatorial reefs*

- **DISTANCE:** 10 or 21 miles (or anything in-between).
- **TERRAIN/DIFFICULTY:** Flat; easy as pie.
- **START:** State historical marker on West Shore Road, near Champlain monument at St. Anne's Shrine.
- **GETTING THERE/PARKING:** From US 2 in South Alburg, take VT 129 to Isle La Motte; from US 2 in Alburg, take West Shore Road to the VT 129 causeway to Isle La Motte. Once on the island follow Shrine Road to the start.

This tour is easily the best for those who like really flat riding or wish to avoid traffic to the greatest extent possible—it would be perfect for a family with small children. The basic loop is fairly short, but can be extended by 2 to 11 miles with additional lakeside riding as you wish. The extension takes Lake Shore Road north toward Alburg and you can continue into the town for food or supplies, or turn around at any point you want.

Isle La Motte was chartered in 1779. Some historians suggest that it was granted along with the Two Heroes (see the regional intro), but state records indicate separate groups of petitioners and independent grants and charters. The former French shrine on the island was not forgotten by the local Indians and the Mohawk called the place *Tgaw-istaniyonteh,* meaning "there a bell is suspended." The town's name was changed to Vineyard in 1802 for unknown reasons, but the original name was restored 28 years later. Interestingly, the Black Sun Vineyards on the island claim to be Vermont's oldest.

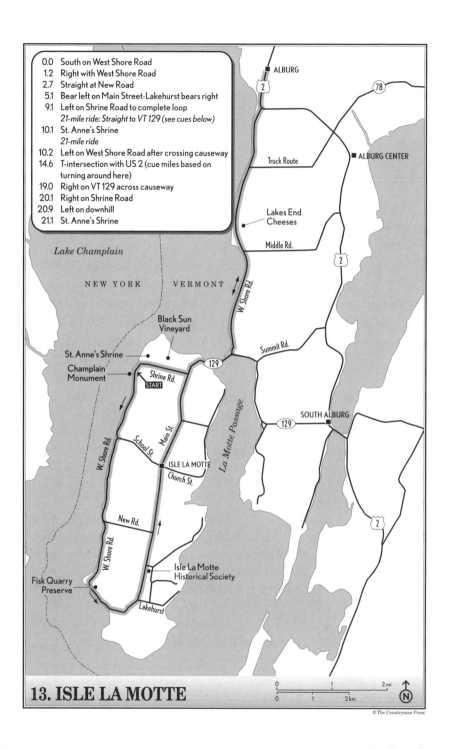

0.0 South on West Shore Road
1.2 Right with West Shore Road
2.7 Straight at New Road
5.1 Bear left on Main Street-Lakehurst bears right
9.1 Left on Shrine Road to complete loop
21-mile ride: Straight to VT 129 (see cues below)
10.1 St. Anne's Shrine
21-mile ride
10.2 Left on West Shore Road after crossing causeway
14.6 T-intersection with US 2 (cue miles based on turning around here)
19.0 Right on VT 129 across causeway
20.1 Right on Shrine Road
20.9 Left on downhill
21.1 St. Anne's Shrine

Lake Champlain

NEW YORK   VERMONT

W. Shore Rd.

ALBURG

Truck Route

ALBURG CENTER

Lakes End Cheeses

Middle Rd.

Black Sun Vineyard

St. Anne's Shrine

Summit Rd.

Champlain Monument

Shrine Rd.
START

Main St.

School St.

La Motte Passage

SOUTH ALBURG

ISLE LA MOTTE

Church St.

New Rd.

W. Shore Rd.

Isle La Motte Historical Society

Fisk Quarry Preserve

Lakehurst

13. ISLE LA MOTTE

0   1   2 mi
0   1   2 km

N

© The Countryman Press

0.0 Ride south on West Shore Road.

1.2 Bear right with West Shore Road.

2.7 Continue straight where New Road is left—if you want to avoid any riding on dirt roads you can turn left here, which reduces the ride by 2.7 miles.

3.6 Surface changes to dirt/gravel.

3.9 There are interesting stone arches as part of the house to the left.

4.0 The Fisk Quarry Preserve is on the left—a short path leads to an abandoned marble quarry, claimed to be the oldest in the state.

Having walked to this quarry I learned that the island possesses history far older than Champlain's claimed landing here. The Chazy or Chazgan reef on the island is the oldest reef anywhere in the world in which corals appear. It was formed some 450–80 million years ago near the equator and brought to its current location by plate tectonics.

5.0 The surface returns to pavement.

5.1 Bear left on Main Street where Lakehurst bears right.

5.6 The Isle La Motte Historical Society is on the right at Quarry Road.

This is a local history museum in an 1830 schoolhouse and a 19th-century blacksmith shop, originally located in the center of town. There are blacksmith tools, photographs, family records, Native American artifacts, and items of local interest. Hours are July and August, Saturday, 1–4 PM—free.

7.3 Village of Isle La Motte with several stone buildings.

9.1 Turn left on Shrine Road to complete the loop.

For 21-mile ride: *ride straight to VT 129 and continue at the cues below.*

9.5 The Black Sun Vineyard is on the right.

9.9 There is a sharp left turn on the downhill.

10.1 St. Anne's Shrine—end of the tour.

21-MILE RIDE

9.8 There is a monument on the right with benches if you want a rest.

10.2 Turn left on West Shore Road after crossing the causeway. This is lovely riding as you are right next to the lake with no intervening houses.

12.6 Lakes End Cheeses is on the right, with farm-made cheeses from both cow and goat milk.

14.6 T-intersection with US 2. US 2 has moderate traffic, but speeds will be relatively slow here in Alburg. You can either reverse to go back to Isle La Motte if you only wanted additional lakeside riding, or turn left on US 2 north for stores and food in Alburg (another .8 mile).

19.0 Turn right on VT 129 across the causeway—this mileage assumes you reversed direction at US 2 in Alburg.

Bundled up early season riders on West Shore Road

20.1 Turn right on Shrine Road.

20.5 The Black Sun Vineyard is on the right.

20.9 There is a sharp left turn on the downhill.

21.1 St. Anne's Shrine—end of the tour.

Gordon Landing–Rouses Point

Blissful lakeside riding in two states
(with a Quebec option)

- **DISTANCE**: 59 or 69 miles.

- **TERRAIN/DIFFICULTY**: Lightly rolling in the Lake Champlain Islands and mostly flat in Quebec and New York; moderate.

- **START**: Gordon Landing ferry landing in Grand Isle, on the Lake Champlain Islands.

- **GETTING THERE/PARKING**: I-89 to Exit 17 (signed for the islands and the NY ferry), follow US 2 West for 10+ miles, then VT 314 signed for the NY ferry. Free parking at the ferry.

This was the very first ride that I did in the Lake Champlain region, a loop that features some of the best lakeside riding in both Vermont and New York. You could ride this in a clockwise direction, but there are two reasons I prefer it this way: cycling east on Cumberland Head gives you great views near the end of the ride, and the ferry trip is a great way to finish the tour.

This ride takes local roads from the ferry landing to the northern end of Grand Isle, where it joins US route 2. US 2 through the Lake Champlain Islands offers superb riding, with lake views and a largely unspoiled rural landscape. North Hero is a pleasant place for a break with its expansive view of the lake and the northern Green Mountains. After crossing to the Alburg peninsula, you soon turn off onto VT 129, which leads to an optional exploration of Isle La Motte (see tour 13). Continuing north along the lakeshore you reach Alburg, which is the decision point for riding the basic loop or adding a brief extension into Quebec. The short loop follows US 2 to Rouses Point and then skirts the lake, while the long option visits the towns of Noyan and Lacolle before turning south. The routes rejoin and enjoy some easy riding on

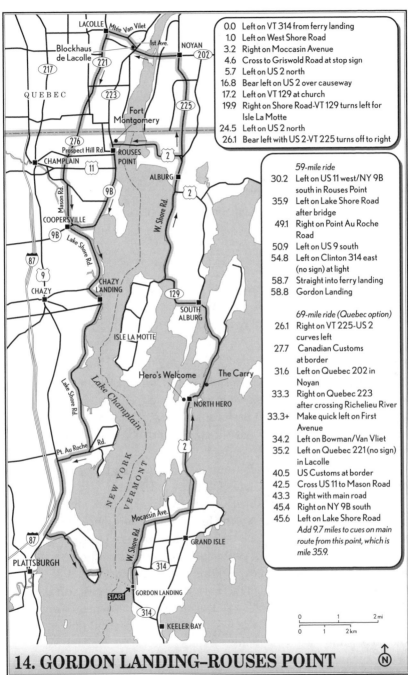

0.0	Left on VT 314 from ferry landing
1.0	Left on West Shore Road
3.2	Right on Moccasin Avenue
4.6	Cross to Griswold Road at stop sign
5.7	Left on US 2 north
16.8	Bear left on US 2 over causeway
17.2	Left on VT 129 at church
19.9	Right on Shore Road-VT 129 turns left for Isle La Motte
24.5	Left on US 2 north
26.1	Bear left with US 2-VT 225 turns off to right

59-mile ride

30.2	Left on US 11 west/NY 9B south in Rouses Point
35.9	Left on Lake Shore Road after bridge
49.1	Right on Point Au Roche Road
50.9	Left on US 9 south
54.8	Left on Clinton 314 east (no sign) at light
58.7	Straight into ferry landing
58.8	Gordon Landing

69-mile ride (Quebec option)

26.1	Right on VT 225-US 2 curves left
27.7	Canadian Customs at border
31.6	Left on Quebec 202 in Noyan
33.3	Right on Quebec 223 after crossing Richelieu River
33.3+	Make quick left on First Avenue
34.2	Left on Bowman/Van Vliet
35.2	Left on Quebec 221 (no sign) in Lacolle
40.5	US Customs at border
42.5	Cross US 11 to Mason Road
43.3	Right with main road
45.4	Right on NY 9B south
45.6	Left on Lake Shore Road
	Add 9.7 miles to cues on main route from this point, which is mile 35.9.

14. GORDON LANDING–ROUSES POINT

the New York shore of the lake, with lakeside riding at Trombly Bay and Monty Bay. A downhill run on US 9 brings you to Cumberland Head and the ferry to close the circle.

0.0 Turn left on VT 314 leaving the ferry landing.

1.0 Turn left on West Shore Road.

3.2 Turn right on Moccasin Avenue.

3.6 There is a very old log cabin on the left.

4.6 Cross to Griswold Road at the stop sign.

5.2 There is an interesting serpentine, low stone wall on the right.

5.7 Turn left on US 2 north.

This road generally has a decent shoulder and I've always found traffic to be very gracious to cyclists here including trucks, which will often cross to the opposite lane if they can.

11.0 There is a restroom at the Hero's Welcome general store and marina in North Hero.

They also have soup and sandwiches; this is a good place to take a break (not that the riding has been strenuous!) with lakefront picnic tables to enjoy the view.

12.5 This narrow stretch of land is called "The Carry," as it provided a short portage from one side of the lake to the other for early travelers in canoes.

16.8 Bear left on US 2 over the causeway. You may have a short delay here if the bridge is up in order to let boats through.

17.2 Turn left on VT 129 at the church.

19.9 Bear right on Shore Road where VT 129 turns left for Isle La Motte.

Option: *If you'd like to visit St. Anne's shrine or add additional mileage by riding a 7- or 12-mile loop around Isle La Motte, see tour 13 for information.*

The next 4 miles are perhaps the most enjoyable shoreline riding anywhere on the lake. The lake is very close to the road at all times and there are no houses or "camps" visually blocking it from the road. There are still a few working farms here, but these are being slowly—and sadly—replaced by new housing.

24.5 Turn left on US 2 north at the southern approach to Alburg. There will be more traffic on US 2 here, but it will be going slowly to meet the village speed limit.

25.3 Alburg—there are stores and food here.

26.1 Bear left with US 2 where VT 225 turns off to the right.

The next 4 miles can be a little busy, but the shoulder is wide here.

For 69-mile ride: *Turn right here for the extension into Quebec and continue at the cues below.*

28.7 Ride up the approach ramp to the bridge over the Richelieu River, which drains Lake Champlain. As you descend from the bridge, you can see the remains of Fort Montgomery on the right.

Due to the continuing American distrust of England after the war of 1812, construction of a fort on a sand spit known as Island Point was started at this strategic location in 1816. However, work was abandoned three years later when it was learned that the site was actually in Canada, giving rise to the name "Fort Blunder." Although the land was eventually ceded to the United States, by then the construction materials had been plundered by locals and incorporated in many Rouses Point structures still in use today. Construction of Fort Montgomery was started in 1844, but not completed until 1870, by which time it really served no purpose. Although armed from the Civil War until early in the 20th century, this fort was never actually garrisoned with troops. When a decision was made to build the Alburg–Rouses Point bridge in 1935, the fort was purchased by the contractor and largely destroyed to reuse the stone for the footings of the new bridge. The remaining small section is privately owned.

30.2 Turn left on US 11 west/NY 9B south in Rouses Point. The Quebec border is just to the right here.

First settled in 1783 and named after early resident Jacques Rouse, Rouses Point was once a major port on the lake. In the mid-19th century, travel between Montreal and Albany was accomplished by train to Rouses Point, lake steamer to Whitehall, and then another train to Albany (and points south). The town prospered as the transfer point between transportation modes, also benefiting from the nearby border. When the rail line from Montreal was extended to Plattsburgh, Rouses Point was soon supplanted as the northern point of call for the steamers, much as it had previously succeeded St. Jean on the Richelieu River when the tracks first crossed the border. Rouses Point's former glory days are witnessed by the grand captain's and merchant's houses seen on the lake-

Avoiding a long detour!

front as you leave town.

35.9 Turn left on Lake Shore Road after crossing the Great Chazy River.

37.7 There is a "penny farthing" (high-wheel bicycle) mailbox constructed of welded chain on the left.

40.5 There are quite a few historical markers along the road in this area, several of them related to Revolutionary era events.

40.9 Chazy Landing—Minor Farm Road leading to the town of Chazy is on the right.

44.5 Trombly Bay is on your left with open views of the lake.

46.4 Monty Bay Marina has a small store, a patio and restrooms.

49.1 Turn right on Point Au Roche Road.

50.9 Turn left on US 9 south.

54.8 Turn left on Clinton 314 east (no sign) at the light, signed for the ferry to Vermont.

55.8 For the next 3 miles the road often follows the shore of Cumberland Bay with fine views.
To the south you can see Valcour Island, where a naval battle fought by Benedict Arnold (before he changed sides) in the early days of the Revolution played an important delaying roll for the American forces.

58.7 Ride straight into the ferry landing and buy your ticket at the booth.

58.8 Gordon Landing—end of the tour.

69-MILE RIDE (QUEBEC OPTION)

26.1 Turn right on VT 225 where US 2 curves left.

27.7 Canadian Customs at the border.

31.6 Turn left on Quebec 202 in Noyan—moderate traffic here.

33.3 Turn right on Quebec 223 after crossing the Richelieu River.

33.3+ Make a quick left on 1st Avenue at an old blockhouse on the left.

34.2 Turn left on Bowman/Van Vliet at a T-intersection.

35.2 Turn left on Quebec 221 (no sign) in Lacolle and stay straight at all crossroads.

There is a Greek restaurant a block to the right at the turn and a French restaurant two blocks to the left on your route. There are other food options in town as well as a "depanneur" (general store).

40.5 US Customs at the border.

42.5 Cross US 11 to Mason Road.

43.3 Bear right with the main road.

45.4 Turn right on NY 9B south at a T-intersection.

45.6 Turn left on Lake Shore Road.

Add 9.7 miles to the cues on the main route from this point, which is mile 35.9.

PLATTSBURGH AND THE NEW YORK NORTHERN TOURS

A peaceful lakefront park in Plattsburgh

PLATTSBURGH IS VERY MUCH a working city, although it is also home to a campus of the State University of New York. There is a fine historic brick business district in the traditional downtown, although much of the city's commercial life has moved to a new strip area on NY 3 near the I-87 interchange. The city and the region were hard hit by the 1995 closing of the Strategic Air Command base in town and still have not fully recovered. However, my experience is that the roads in the region are well maintained and generally have light traffic outside of the immediate Plattsburgh area. Apparently the highway budget does not include county road signs (maybe it was all blown on asphalt?), as I am hard pressed to find any in Clinton County while neighboring Essex County does an excellent job in this area. The northeastern corner of the state is generally quite flat, but the foothills of the Adirondacks are not far to the west of Plattsburgh.

Plattsburgh was once in New France, part of the land grants made by Louis XV in 1711 to "place under cultivation and to locate settlers on them," but the French were not successful in actually settling the region. This area was ceded to the British at the end of the French and Indian, or Seven Years' War. The first real settlement was in 1766 by Count Charles de Fredenburgh, who had received a large grant and built a sawmill near where the Saranac River joins Lake Champlain. However, he and his family were forced to flee to Canada at the onset of the Revolution.

Benedict Arnold and the fledgling American navy were defeated by the British at the Battle of Lake Champlain, which began off Valcour Island on October 11, 1776, and ended two days later with all of the new American fleet captured or scuttled. However, historians generally agree that this gave the American forces a chance to recover over the winter and defeat General Burgoyne at Saratoga the following summer. In 1784 Zepheniah Platt and others came to the region and purchased the former Fredenburgh grant, forming the town of Plattsburgh the following year.

The town gained military importance with the outbreak of the War of 1812, when it became a major staging area for the campaigns north of the border. A week of minor ground engagements with the approaching British army led up to the decisive Battle of Plattsburgh on September 11, 1814, when a smaller American naval force defeated a much larger British one in Cumberland Bay; there is a towering obelisk downtown commemorating this event. This victory caused the British to halt the advance and return to Canada, thereby turning the tide of the war.

One of my favorite places in the Plattsburgh area is the large collection of outdoor sculpture on the SUNY campus. The school also houses the Plattsburgh Art Museum. There are some fine houses near the lakefront in the older part of town and this area can provide some pleasant riding. The Amtrak "Adirondack" still stops daily at the handsome, century-old Delaware & Hudson train station near the lake.

Most of the hotels and motels are very close to the interchange of NY 3 and I-87 (Exit 37). There are also a number of chain and local restaurants in this area, but my personal pick for dining is Irises Café and Wine Bar in the old downtown.

Tourism Info

Plattsburgh North Country Chamber of Commerce, 7061 Route 9, Plattsburgh (518-563-1000 or chamber@westelcom.com)

Bike Shops

Dannemora—Steve's Bike Shop, 986 Route 374 (518-492-2685; 888-313-2995 or info@nolimits-sbs.com)

Plattsburgh—Maui North, 31 Durkee Street (518-563-7245 or mauinorth@westelcom.com)

Plattsburgh—Viking Ski & Cycle, 453 Route 3 (518-561-5539 or viking@westelcom.com)

Plattsburgh—Wooden Ski & Wheel, 4614 Route 9 South (518-561-2790 or wooden @westelcom.com)

15

Champlain–Chazy

Mooers, some cows, apples, and the lake

- **DISTANCE**: 34, 42, or 50 miles
- **TERRAIN/DIFFICULTY**: Generally flat to lightly rolling; easy
- **START**: Paquette Park in Champlain
- **GETTING THERE/PARKING**: I-87 to Exit 42, east on US 11 to US 9 north into Champlain. Paquette Park will be on the right at the bottom of the hill.

These rides are in the far northeastern corner of New York State, where there is an excellent network of well-paved and generally lightly traveled roads. Champlain could best be described as one of those towns that is down on its luck. It's clear that it used to be a much busier place before the Northway was built, when a steady stream of traffic passed though on the way to or from the nearby border crossing. There isn't much "downtown" here except for a bar (the last country store closed several years ago), but there are services at the intersection of US 9 and US 11 just south of town.

Leaving Champlain you quickly find yourself on very quiet roads heading west to Mooers, another town whose glory days are past. From there you have three choices of routes, with all of them providing pleasant riding. Besides the number of miles, the main determining factor here is that the two longer routes offer some wonderful riding along the lake, while those on the short ride will mostly see it from a distance. However, those interested in local history may select the short loop as it passes near the Miner Museum in Chazy. There is also a 6-mile extension into Rouses Point near the end of the ride that provides additional lake views. Revolutionary War–minded riders will note the abundance of historical markers in this area, which Benadict Arnold and Benjamin Franklin, among others, passed through in their travels.

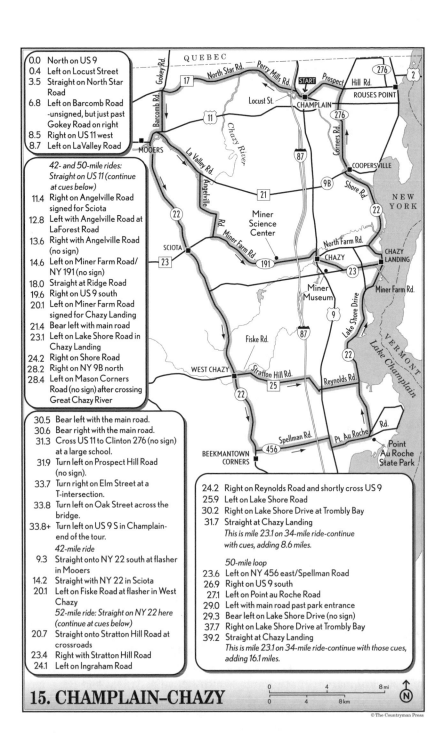

0.0	North on US 9
0.4	Left on Locust Street
3.5	Straight on North Star Road
6.8	Left on Barcomb Road -unsigned, but just past Gokey Road on right
8.5	Right on US 11 west
8.7	Left on LaValley Road

42- and 50-mile rides: Straight on US 11 (continue at cues below)

11.4	Right on Angelville Road signed for Sciota
12.8	Left with Angelville Road at LaForest Road
13.6	Right with Angelville Road (no sign)
14.6	Left on Miner Farm Road/ NY 191 (no sign)
18.0	Straight at Ridge Road
19.6	Right on US 9 south
20.1	Left on Miner Farm Road signed for Chazy Landing
21.4	Bear left with main road
23.1	Left on Lake Shore Road in Chazy Landing
24.2	Right on Shore Road
28.2	Right on NY 9B north
28.4	Left on Mason Corners Road (no sign) after crossing Great Chazy River

30.5	Bear left with the main road.
30.6	Bear right with the main road.
31.3	Cross US 11 to Clinton 276 (no sign) at a large school.
31.9	Turn left on Prospect Hill Road (no sign).
33.7	Turn right on Elm Street at a T-intersection.
33.8	Turn left on Oak Street across the bridge.
33.8+	Turn left on US 9 S in Champlain- end of the tour.

42-mile ride

9.3	Straight onto NY 22 south at flasher in Mooers
14.2	Straight with NY 22 in Sciota
20.1	Left on Fiske Road at flasher in West Chazy

52-mile ride: Straight on NY 22 here (continue at cues below)

20.7	Straight onto Stratton Hill Road at crossroads
23.4	Right with Stratton Hill Road
24.1	Left on Ingraham Road

24.2	Right on Reynolds Road and shortly cross US 9
25.9	Left on Lake Shore Road
30.2	Right on Lake Shore Drive at Trombly Bay
31.7	Straight at Chazy Landing

This is mile 23.1 on 34-mile ride-continue with cues, adding 8.6 miles.

50-mile loop

23.6	Left on NY 456 east/Spellman Road
26.9	Right on US 9 south
27.1	Left on Point au Roche Road
29.0	Left with main road past park entrance
29.3	Bear left on Lake Shore Drive (no sign)
37.7	Right on Lake Shore Drive at Trombly Bay
39.2	Straight at Chazy Landing

This is mile 23.1 on 34-mile ride-continue with those cues, adding 16.1 miles.

15. CHAMPLAIN–CHAZY

0		4		8 mi
0		4		8 km

N

0.0 Ride north on US 9.

0.4 Turn left on Locust Street.

0.7 You are now on Perry Mills Road as the Great Chazy River appears on your left.

3.5 Continue straight on North Star Road.

6.8 Turn left on Barcomb Road—unsigned, but just past Gokey Road on the right.

8.5 Turn right on US 11 west at a T-intersection.

8.7 Turn left on LaValley Road, which follows the Great Chazy River.
For 42- and 52-mile rides: Ride straight here on US 11 and continue at cues below.

10.8 There is a sweet old barn on the left.

11.4 Turn right on Angelville Road signed for Sciota.

12.8 Turn left with Angelville Road at LaForest Road.

13.6 Turn right with Angelville Road (no sign).

14.6 Turn left on Miner Farm Road/NY 191 (no sign) at a T-intersection.

18.0 Straight at Ridge Road and soon cross over I-87.

19.6 Turn right on US 9 south at a T-intersection.

19.7 Enter the town of Chazy, situated on the Little Chazy River.
The town was named for Lt. de Chézy, who was killed near here in a 1666 raid by the Iroquois. Jean Laframboise was the first white settler in this area, but he was driven off in 1777 by Burgoyne's army and his house destroyed. He returned in 1783 and became the first apple grower in a region that now claims the world's largest MacIntosh orchard, producing some quarter million boxes of apples a year.

William Miner was another important resident, a wealthy industrialist and philanthropist who created a fortune from the invention of what became the standard railroad coupler. Starting in 1902 with a 146-acre farm owned by an uncle, he quickly built "Heart's Delight Farm" into a huge modern, model farming operation that had electricity before the Governor's Mansion in Albany. His legacy is the W. H. Miner Agricultural Research

Institute (you passed it 2 miles back), which continues to develop and teach the best practices in dairy farming, equine management and environmental conservation.

20.1 Turn left on Miner Farm Road signed for Chazy Landing.

Option: *Continue a short ways to visit the Alice T. Miner Museum (518-846-7336), which has 15 rooms of period furniture and other furnishings in a restored 19th-century house. The museum also contains salesmen's sample miniature furniture, a china collection, porcelain and glass, textiles, dolls, and other early Americana. Alice Miner was a champion of the Colonial revivalist movement and opened her museum in 1924, managing it for a quarter century until her death. The museum is open Tuesday through Saturday from 10 AM to 4 PM with guided tours at 10:00, 11:30, 1:00, and 2:30; admission fee.*

21.4 Bear left with the main road.

23.1 Turn left on Lake Shore Road at a T-intersection in Chazy Landing.

24.2 Bear right on Shore Road where North Farm Road is left.

26.4 There is a "penny farthing" (high-wheel bicycle) welded chain mailbox on the right.

28.2 Turn right on NY 9B north at a T-intersection.

28.4 Turn left on Mason Corners Road (no sign) after crossing the Great Chazy River.

Option: *Continue on NY 9B for a 6.2-mile extension that takes you through Rouses Point; see cues at end.*

30.5 Bear left with the main road.

30.6 Bear right with the main road.

31.3 Cross US 11 to Clinton 276 (no sign) at a large school.

31.9 Turn left on Prospect Hill Road (no sign).

33.7 Turn right on Elm Street at a T-intersection.

33.8 Turn left on Oak Street across the bridge.

33.8+ Turn left on US 9 in Champlain—end of the tour.

42-MILE RIDE

9.3 Straight onto NY 22 south at the flasher in Mooers. This road has smooth pavement and an excellent shoulder.

Mooers is named after Major General Benjamin Mooers, who fought in the Revolution and settled at Point au Roche in 1783 with other veterans. He later led the local militia in the defense of Plattsburgh during the War of 1812 and became a state senator. The largely vacant commercial buildings at this intersection are a sad reminder of long past better days for Mooers.

14.2 Straight with NY 22 in Sciota.

20.1 Turn left on Fiske Road at a flasher in West Chazy.

For 52-mile ride: *Ride straight on NY 22 here and continue at the cues below.*

20.7 Straight onto Stratton Hill Road at the crossroad.

Unicyclist in Chazy

23.4 Turn right with Stratton Hill Road at a T-intersection.

24.1 Turn left on Ingraham Road.

24.2 Turn right on Reynolds Road and shortly cross US 9.

25.9 Turn left on Lake Shore Road at a T-intersection.

26.2 Monty Bay Marina is on the right—restrooms, small store and deck with lake view.

30.2 Bear right on Lake Shore Drive at Trombly Bay.

31.7 Straight at Chazy Landing—Miner Farm Road for Chazy is on the left. *This is mile 23.1 on the 34-mile ride. Continue with those cues and add 8.6 miles to them.*

50-MILE LOOP

23.6 Turn left on NY 456 east/Spellman Road.

25.5 There are views of Mount Mansfield and Camel's Hump ahead to the right.

26.9 Turn right on US 9 south at a T-intersection.

27.1 Turn left on Point au Roche Road.

29.0 Turn left with the main road just past the entrance to Point au Roche State Park.

29.3 Bear left on Lake Shore Drive (no sign).

33.7 Monty Bay Marina on the right—restrooms, small store, and deck with lake view.

37.7 Bear right on Lake Shore Drive at Trombly Bay.

39.2 Straight at Chazy Landing—Miner Farm Road for Chazy is on the left. *This is mile 23.1 on the 34-mile ride. Continue with those cues and add 16.1 miles to them.*

ROUSES POINT EXTENSION

(See tour 14 for information on Rouses Point.)

33.5 Turn left on Clinton 276 north/Pratt Street in Rouses Point.

34.0 Turn left on Church Street at a T-intersection.

34.2 Turn right on Prospect Hill Road (no sign) at a T-intersection.

36.1 Cross Clinton 276, which clearly winds around a lot.

37.9 Turn right on Elm Street at a T-intersection.

40.0 Turn left on Oak Street across the bridge.

40.0+ Turn left on US 9—end of the tour.

16

Plattsburgh–Dannemora

Into the (foot) hills

- **DISTANCE:** 46 or 59 miles
- **TERRAIN/DIFFICULTY:** Lightly to seriously rolling with two major climbs on the short route and rolling to mountainous with three major climbs on the long. Moderately difficult for the short loop, challenging on the long ride.
- **START:** Maui North bike shop at 31 Durkee Street in Plattsburgh. The Farmers Market across the street is open on Saturday 9–3 in season.
- **GETTING THERE/PARKING:** I-87 to Exit 37, NY 3 east for a mile and a half, turn right on City Hall Place to Durkee Street. Plenty of free parking across from the start.

Although there is certainly some pleasant scenery on these loops, I would have to say that this tour is generally more about the cycling, with some points of cultural and historic interest. The long ride in particular has a lot of climbing (and is the second most challenging ride in this book), but they both have ascents that will test your fortitude. However, as my parents told my brother and I when we were riding our first tours on our own bikes (instead of sitting comfortably on the back of theirs), "what goes up must go down." Each loop has a 12-mile segment near the end that is almost all downhill, bringing you back to lake level from the heights of Dannemora. There is an optional short ride at the end to visit the large outdoor sculpture collection at SUNY, Plattsburgh, which is highly recommended. You could alternately walk around the sculpture before or after the ride, and there is also a worthwhile art museum on the campus.

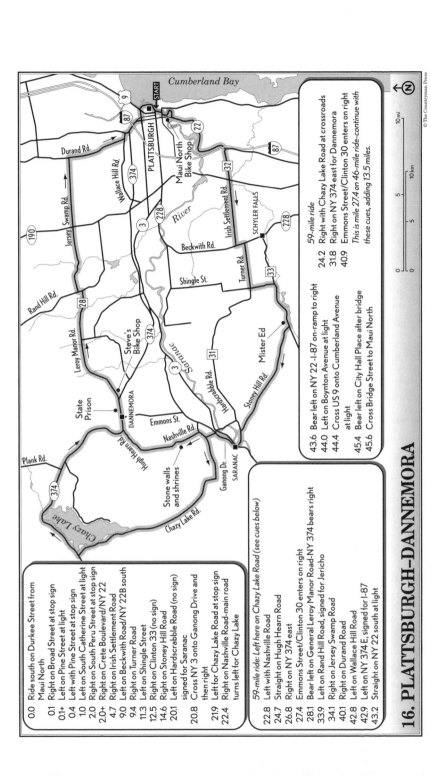

16. PLATTSBURGH–DANNEMORA

0.0	Ride south on Durkee Street from Maui North
0.1	Right on Broad Street at stop sign
0.1+	Left on Pine Street at light
0.4	Left with Pine Street at stop sign
1.0	Left on South Catherine Street at light
2.0	Right on South Peru Street at stop sign
2.0+	Right on Crete Boulevard/NY 22
4.7	Right on Irish Settlement Road
9.0	Left on Beckwith Road/NY 22B south
9.4	Right on Turner Road
11.3	Left on Shingle Street
12.5	Right on Clinton 33 (no sign)
14.6	Right on Stoney Hill Road
20.1	Left on Hardscrabble Road (no sign) signed for Saranac
20.8	Cross NY 3 onto Ganong Drive and then right
21.9	Left for Chazy Lake Road at stop sign
22.4	Right on Nashville Road–main road turns left for Chazy Lake

59-mile ride: Left here on Chazy Lake Road (see cues below)

22.8	Left with Nashville Road
24.7	Straight on Hugh Hearn Road
26.8	Right on NY 374 east
27.4	Emmons Street/Clinton 30 enters on right
28.1	Bear left on General Leroy Manor Road–NY 374 bears right
33.9	Left on Rand Hill Road, signed for Jericho
34.1	Right on Jersey Swamp Road
40.1	Right on Durand Road
42.8	Left on Wallace Hill Road
42.9	Left on NY 374 E, signed for I-87
43.2	Straight on NY 22 south at light

43.6	Bear left on NY 22–I-87 on-ramp to right
44.0	Left on Boynton Avenue at light
44.4	Cross US 9 onto Cumberland Avenue at light
45.4	Bear left on City Hall Place after bridge
45.6	Cross Bridge Street to Maui North

59-mile ride:

24.2	Right with Chazy Lake Road at crossroads
31.8	Right on NY 374 east for Dannemora
40.9	Emmons Street/Clinton 30 enters on right
	This is mile 27.4 on 46-mile ride-continue with these cues, adding 13.5 miles.

0.0 Ride south on Durkee Street from Maui North.

0.1 Turn right on Broad Street at the stop sign.

0.1+ Turn left on Pine Street at the light—the Saranac River is on your left.

0.4 Turn left with Pine Street at the stop sign.

1.0 Turn left on South Catherine Street at the light.

2.0 Turn right on South Peru Street at the stop sign—signed for NY 22 South.

2.0+ Turn right on Crete Boulevard at the sign for NY 22 South—there's a wide shoulder here.

2.5 Former Plattsburgh Air Force Base is on the left, which was closed in 1995.

4.7 Turn right on Irish Settlement Road after crossing I-87.
The next 4 miles are arrow straight and descend gradually almost the entire way—or is that just an illusion?

9.0 Turn left on Beckwith Road/NY 22B south at a T-intersection.

9.4 Turn right on Turner Road.

11.3 Turn left on Shingle Street at a T-intersection.

12.5 Turn right on Clinton 33 (no sign) at a T-intersection.

12.9 Macomb State Park is on the left.

14.4 Ed the horse is resting at the fence on the right.

14.6 Turn right on Stoney Hill Road. You have a 1.5-mile climb and then things get easier.

16.1 Start of rougher pavement.

17.7 Start of long and sometimes steep downhill into Saranac. Use caution and keep your speed down due to the rough surface in places.

19.3 A wide view opens up and you can see the prison at 2 o'clock.

20.1 Turn left on Hardscrabble Road (no sign) signed for Saranac.

20.8 Cross NY 3 onto Ganong Drive and bear right.

21.9 Turn left for Chazy Lake Road at a stop sign.

22.4 Turn right on Nashville Road where the main road turns left for Chazy Lake.

There's a unique "periscope" lookout on the house at the turn.

For 59-mile ride: *Turn left here on Chazy Lake Road and continue at cues below.*

22.8 Turn left with Nashville Road.

The next 3 miles are largely uphill, although there are brief breaks.

23.8 Look for very carefully squared stone walls and several shrines on the left.

These are easier to see in the spring or fall. They are a continuing labor of love for Agnes Cornelius, who lives with her mother in the house that quickly comes up on the left. If you're interested in exploring her rock work, she has given permission for riders to lean their bike against the garage by the road and walk around the grounds. She started in 1985 after pulling a layer of loam off a century-old wall and being fascinated by the revealed stones underneath. She describes her work as a process of folding, as she removes large rounded stones from the collapsed wall to get to the smaller stones with squared edges that she finds toward the middle of the old wall. Then she carefully rebuilds the wall, first using the rounded stones and then covering them with the more sharply chiseled ones to form the smooth outer surface. I walked on one precisely formed wall that was some 12 feet wide and well over a yard high. There are other sculptural objects spread around the grounds.

24.7 Straight on Hugh Hearn Road where Nashville Road turns right.

26.8 Turn right on NY 374 east (sign after the turn) at a T-intersection.

27.0 Most riders will probably need to brake to meet the posted 30-mph speed limit entering Dannemora!

Iron ore was discovered near here about 1831 and the following year several business-men of the area entered into partnership to mine the ore. Most of the land in the region was owned by a Plattsburgh lawyer named John Skinner. It was he who selected the name Dannemora when the western part of Beekmantown was split off in 1854. The name derives from a Swedish town with a large iron ore field near Stockholm, being a combination of "Danne" for early Danish settlers in Sweden and "Mora" for a region known for spruce trees in Sweden.

Descending at speed

27.4 Emmons Street/Clinton 30 enters right near the start of the prison wall. *Dannemora is about the only option for food on the route. Locally recommended Ting's diner is located just as you reach the prison wall, and there is also a convenience store nearby.*

The location of the prison at Dannemora has an interesting history. New York had built the first state prisons at Auburn and Sing Sing in the 1820s, but cheap convict labor allowed prison goods to be sold for half the price of those made on the outside, which caused bitter feelings in a period of economic depression. When New York realized that another state prison was required, it was decided that the focus would be on the mining and smelting of iron ore, which would be less disruptive of private enterprise. Dannemora gives inmates a lot more freedom than most prisons and it appears that the basis for it may go back a very long ways. Dannemora resident Rod Bigelow's site (http://bigelowsociety.com/slic/dann1.htm) has a circa 1871 photograph depicting

Pride's Shanty, showing an elderly inmate sitting in front of his small private house built on prison grounds. It seems likely that inmates were allowed to build small gardens at some point early in the 20th century. Starting around 1930 a grid of terraces was built on a sloping piece of land known as the "courts." These are now formally "leased" to groups of inmates, who are allowed an amazing range of latitude in what they do here, which includes, "to garden, to cook and eat, to play cards, checkers and chess: in a word, to socialize." There were even a ski jump and toboggan run on the grounds at one point.

28.1 Bear left on General Leroy Manor Road where NY 374 bears right.
Steve's Bike Shop is right at the fork. Begin your descent back to lake level as most of the next 12 miles is downhill.

33.9 Turn left on Rand Hill Road, signed for Jericho, at a T-intersection.
I regret this brief uphill interlude, but it brings you to 6 more miles of downhill riding.

34.1 Turn right on Jersey Swamp Road.

40.1 Turn right on Durand Road at a T-intersection.

42.8 Turn left on Wallace Hill Road at a T-intersection.

42.9 Turn left on NY 374 E, signed for I-87. The next mile can be challenging due to the I-87 interchange, but you should be fine if you stay in the correct lane for NY 22 and signal your intentions.

43.2 Ride in the lane for NY 22 south at the light. You can move over to the right lane after passing the I-87 on-ramp just past the light.

43.6 Bear left on NY 22 where there's another I-87 on-ramp to the right.

44.0 Turn left on Boynton Avenue at the light.

44.4 Cross US 9 onto Cumberland Avenue at the light, where there is a sprawling Georgia-Pacific paper plant on the left.

44.9 On the left is a house with a child's playhouse built as a replica.

45.2 There's an attractive small park on the left with a Champlain monument, benches and lake view.

45.2+ The Kent DeLord House Museum (518-561-1035) is on the right at 17 Cumberland Avenue.

Guided tours are held Tuesday–Saturday, noon–4 PM; admission fee.

45.3 A historic (1888) pedestrian suspension bridge is on the left.

45.4 Bear left on City Hall Place after crossing the bridge over the railroad track.

On the left is the towering Macdonough obelisk monument commemorating the Battle of Plattsburgh, when a smaller US fleet defeated the British on September 11, 1814. See tour 4 for information on Thomas Macdonough.

45.6 Cross Bridge Street to Maui North—end of the tour.

59-MILE RIDE

22.4 The next 4 miles are climbing, while the following 5 miles provide a great descent.

24.2 Turn right with Chazy Lake Road at the crossroads.

29.5 Chazy Lake appears on the right.
This is a large lake and you will have glimpses of it for the next several miles.

31.8 Turn right on NY 374 east for Dannemora.
The next 5 miles are rolling but generally downhill.

36.5 Continue on NY 374 where Plank Road joins on the left.
In about half a mile you will begin a stiff 2-mile-long climb.

39.1 Top of the climb and start of a steep descent into Dannemora.

40.9 Emmons Street/Clinton 30 enters right near the start of the prison wall.
This is mile 27.4 on the 46-mile ride. Continue with those cues and add 13.5 miles to them.

OPTIONAL VISIT TO OUTDOOR SCULPTURE AT THE STATE UNIVERSITY OF NEW YORK, PLATTSBURGH

0.0 Continue on Durkee Street from Maui North.

0.1 Turn right on Broad Street at the stop sign.

0.1+ Stay straight on Broad Street at Pine Street.

0.4 Stay straight on Broad Street at South Catherine Street.

0.6 Turn left on Rugar Street at the light.

0.7 Turn right into the parking area at SUNY Plattsburgh.

0.8 Plattsburgh Art Museum is on the left—continue straight into the campus to tour the many pieces of outdoor sculpture (a guide to the sculpture is available in the museum). Return by retracing your route.

17

South Plattsburgh–Peru

Apple orchards, pinewoods,
and mountain views

- **DISTANCE**: 19, 25, or 46 miles.

- **TERRAIN/DIFFICULTY**: Generally lightly rolling on the short rides and moderately rolling on the long loop; easy for the short tours and moderate for the long.

- **START**: Junction of NY 22 and Salmon River Road in South Plattsburgh.

- **GETTING THERE/PARKING**: I-87 to Exit 36, then drive south on NY 22 just over a mile to Salmon River Road (signed for Schuyler Falls) and park on the other side of NY 22. There is a small parking area here with a sheltered picnic table.

The long and short rides share the same beginning and ending, but are dramatically different in between. The long ride has much more climbing, while also bringing you closer to the Adirondacks and providing better views of them. NY 22 has light traffic and a good shoulder as you ride south to Peru. From here the short loops enter an area with a large concentration of apple orchards, which would make them a delight in the spring (mid-May). If you're riding in September you may see palletized open crates distributed among the trees, ready to receive the harvest. You have easy riding back to the start on largely flat roads. The long ride continues south from Peru before turning west and then north, looping around a large mountainous expanse with few interior roads. Turning east, the route soon gains the valley of the Salmon River, which it follows all the way back to the start.

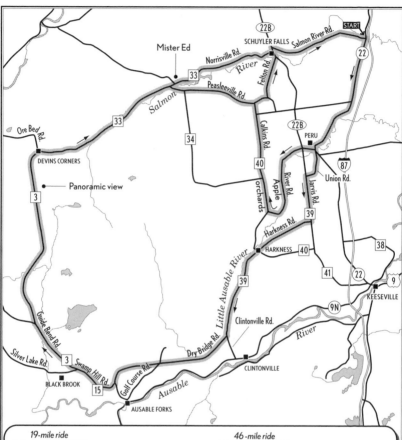

19-mile ride

0.0	South on NY 22
4.7	Left with NY 22 south at flasher in Peru
4.9	Right on Pleasant Street (sign after turn)
5.4	Left on River Road (not sharp left)
8.8	Right on Calkins Road
13.0	Right on Felton Road
	25-mile ride: Left on Peasleeville Road (see cues below)
13.5	Left with Felton Road signed for Schuyler Falls
15.1	Left on NY 22B north (no sign) in Schuyler Falls
15.5	Right on Salmon River Road
18.0	Cross Turnpike Ext. at flasher
19.4	Cross NY 22

25-mile ride

13.5	Right with Peasleeville Road
16.4	Sharply right onto Norrisville Road at store
20.9	Left on NY 22B north (no sign)
21.1	Right on Salmon River Road
25.0	Cross NY 22 to start

46-mile ride

0.0	South on NY 22
4.7	Left with NY 22 south at flasher in Peru
5.0	Right on Union Road just after bridge
6.2	Left on Jarvis Road
7.9	Right on Harkness Road
13.6	Straight on Dry Bridge Road (signed for Ausable Forks)
16.7	Straight-main road bears left (no sign)
19.0	Right on Swamp Hill Road at stop sign
21.1	Right on Guide Bond Road (signed for Fern Lake)
30.5	Right on Peasleeville Road (signed for Peasleeville)
36.7	Left on Norrisville Road at country store
41.2	Left on NY 22B north (no sign) in Schuyler Falls
41.4	Right on Salmon River Road
43.9	Cross Turnpike Ext. at flasher
45.3	Cross NY 22 to start

17. SOUTH PLATTSBURGH–PERU

© The Countryman Press

19-MILE RIDE

0.0 Ride south on NY 22 and immediately cross the Salmon River.

2.7 Bear right with NY 22 south.

4.7 Turn left with NY 22 south at the flasher in Peru.

4.9 Turn right on NY 22B/Pleasant Street (sign after turn) just before the bridge and then bear right where Elm Street forks left.

5.4 Turn left on River Road—not a sharp left on Jarvis.
The next 3 miles are very pleasant riding, with the river valley on the left and orchards or cornfields on the right.

8.8 Turn right on Calkins Road and continue straight at all crossroads.
There are many apple orchards over the next several miles.

13.0 Turn right on Felton Road at a T-intersection.
For 25-mile ride: *Turn left on Peasleeville Road at this intersection and continue at cues below.*

13.5 Turn left with Felton Road signed for Schuyler Falls.
Note the dark brown stone house almost hidden by the trees at the turn. After the turn, you have a clear view of the northern Green Mountains, with the distinctive profiles of Camel's Hump and Mount Mansfield bracketing the city of Burlington.

15.1 Turn left on NY 22B north (no sign) at a T-intersection in Schuyler Falls. There is an old gristmill at the turn.

15.5 Turn right on Salmon River Road and it's all downhill from here as you follow the river back to the start.

18.0 Cross Turnpike Ext. at the flasher.

19.4 Cross NY 22—end of the tour.

25-MILE RIDE

13.5 Bear right with Peasleeville Road.

16.4 Turn sharply right onto Norrisville Road at the country store.

20.9 Turn left on NY 22B north (no sign) at a T-intersection.

21.1 Turn right on Salmon River Road.

25.0 Cross NY 22—end of the tour.

46-MILE RIDE

0.0 Ride south on NY 22 and immediately cross the Salmon River.

2.7 Bear right with NY 22 south.

4.7 Turn left with NY 22 south at the flasher in Peru.
Note: Peru has the last store on the long route for the next 32 miles!

5.0 Turn right on Union Road just after the bridge and quickly enter farm and orchard country.

6.2 Turn left on Jarvis Road at a T-intersection.

6.7 The Northern Orchard farm stand is on the left at an apple-painted barn.

7.9 Turn right on Harkness Road.

10.2 Continue straight at the crossroad in Harkness.

13.6 Ride straight on Dry Bridge Road (signed for Ausable Forks).

16.7 Straight where the main road bears left (no sign).

18.3 Whiteface Mountain is straight ahead in the distance—you can recognize it by the large scar on the side you are facing.

19.0 Turn right on Swamp Hill Road at the stop sign, signed for Black Brook—there is a stiff climb ahead.
Note: You can optionally turn left here for Ausable Forks and food, although you do more descending which you will later have to regain.

21.1 Bear right on Guide Bond Road (signed for Fern Lake).

22.7 Caution—brake on the downhill for a raised lip on the bridge at the bottom of the descent.

Downhill leading to the Salmon River valley on Peasleeville Road

24 Birch trees become more dominant as you enter a different environment from the solid pine forest that you've been in.

29.5 There is a near 360-degree panorama from the top of the hill—you might want to lean your bike against the fence to savor it for a bit.

30.5 Bear right on Peasleeville Road (signed for Peasleeville).

31 Enjoy a steep downhill to the valley of the Salmon River, which you will generally follow back to the start.

36.7 Turn left on Norrisville Road at a large country store.

37.0 Mister Ed is on the left, placidly peering over the fence.

38.6 Macomb State Park is on the right.

41.2 Turn left on NY 22B north (no sign) at a T-intersection in Schuyler Falls.

41.4 Turn right on Salmon River Road and it's all downhill from here as you follow the river back to the start.

43.9 Cross Turnpike Ext. at the flasher.

45.3 Cross NY 22—end of the tour.

ESSEX, WESTPORT, AND THE NEW YORK CENTRAL TOURS

The village of Essex from the Charlotte ferry on an early autumn morning

ALTHOUGH BOTH ARE SMALL, Essex and Westport are interesting destinations in their own right as well as providing a good starting point for a bike ride. Chartered in 1765, Essex was one of the earlier settlements on the New York shore of the lake. However, its early progress was halted when General Burgoyne burned it to the ground en route to his eventual defeat at Saratoga.

It revived in the early 1800s as a center for shipbuilding, mining and transportation, as Essex was situated on the primary trade route between the new republic and Canada. The opening of the Champlain Canal in 1823, offering a direct connection between the lake and the Hudson River, only increased its importance and wealth. However, the coming of the railroads in the second half of the century heavily cut into the former dependence on maritime shipping. Toward the end of the 1800s the village became a popular summer resort and has once again moved in that direction a century later. Essex has one of the best preserved collections of pre–Civil War structures in the country, with the entire village listed on the National Register of Historic Places, and walking tour guide booklets are available at the town office.

Westport had a very similar history, first achieving success as a port for shipping out the natural resources of the Adirondacks, as well as local agricultural and manufactured goods. The railroad age also reduced its importance in Lake Champlain shipping, but the village became a summer destination for the well-heeled from New York City, Albany, and Boston. Although lacking the architectural richness of Essex, Westport is still a quiet and lovely town where there are public concerts at the bandstand on summer evenings. There are several inns and B&Bs providing lodging as well as opportunities for dining in most price ranges. However, what you won't find in either community is anything approaching fast food or convenience stores, so be ready for a more relaxed pace of life.

Although comprised of small communities, this region is not without culture. Westport's Depot Theatre is located in the old train station and gives performances through the summer months, while the Essex Theater Company performs in July and August in the Masonic Lodge next to the ferry landing. The Meadowmount School of Music lies between the villages of Lewis and Wadhams, not far from either Essex or Westport. This music camp was founded in 1944 and offers a summer program for aspiring professional string players and pianists. Yo-Yo Ma and Itzhak Perlman are among the famed musicians who have attended this camp. Check locally for their schedule of performances.

Tourism Info

Essex (www.essexnewyork.com or www.essexny.net)

Westport Chamber of Commerce (518-962-8383 or www.westportny.com)

Adirondack Coast (www.lakechamplainregion.com)

Bike Shops

These small villages cannot support bike shops and the nearest ones are in Plattsburgh, Lake Placid, or Glens Falls. Due to this, make certain that your bike is in good condition before starting any of the rides in this region.

18

Keeseville–Jay

Ladder loops along the Ausable

- **DISTANCE:** 13, 27, 35, or 43 miles.

- **TERRAIN/DIFFICULTY:** Generally lightly rolling on the shortest ride and moderately to seriously rolling on the longer loops; easy on the short loop, moderately difficult on the others, with the difficulty increasing with the length.

- **START:** Front Street/US 9 in Keeseville, across from Adirondack Hardware.

- **GETTING THERE/PARKING:** I-87 to Exit 34, NY 9N east to Keeseville. Lots of free parking is available in town.

This would be a great tour for a group with varying riding abilities or tastes, as there are four variations with a mileage option for everyone. Since all of the loops share a common road on the return, stronger or faster riders could do the longer rides and meet up with friends for the ride back. I term these ladder loops because the outbound and inbound sections resemble ladder legs, while the bridges over the Ausable River determine which rung you cross and the distance of your ride.

The early history of Keeseville is difficult to extract from that of surrounding towns, although it is known that there were two Quaker meetinghouses in a nearby area known as "The Union." Around 1806, Captain Jonathan Bigelow built a dam and then a sawmill on the Ausable River, realizing that the valley was a promising location for manufacturing. Two other men bought the property and added a gristmill, but in 1812 one of them sold his interest to John Keese, who was joined by his brother Richard and the town acquired its current name. By the 1820s the town had grown substantially and industries of all

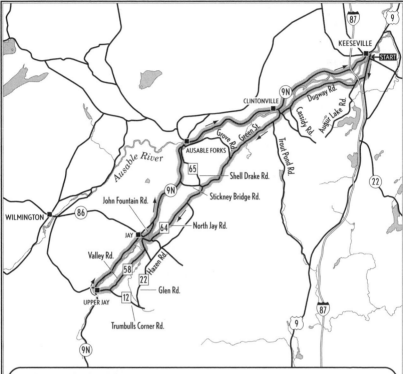

0.0	South on US 9/Front Street up hill
0.9	Right on Augur Lake Road/Essex 15
1.6	Right on Dugway Road
5.6	Right with Dugway Road
6.2	Left on Green Street
	13-mile ride: Right on Dugway Road (continue with cues below)
9.8	Straight on Green Street-Grove Road on right
12.2	Left on North Jay Road
	27-mile ride: Right on Stickney Bridge Road (see cues below)
16.8	Left on Glen Road/Essex 22 at bridge in Jay
	35-mile ride: Right across 1-lane bridge in Jay (see cues below)
17.4	Right on Valley Road/Essex 58
20.2	Right on Trumbull Corners Road/Essex 12
21.0	Right on NY 9N north/Essex 12 in Upper Jay
21.1	Right with NY 9N-Essex 12 turns left
24.8	Straight on NY 9N-Essex 86 is left in Jay
30.6	Left with NY 9N entering Ausable Forks
30.9	Right with NY 9N in Ausable Forks

41.5	Pass under US 87
42.2	Right on Ausable Street in Keeseville
42.8	Right on Main Street
42.9	Right on Front Street/US 9 south at flasher
43.0	*Start*
	35-mile ride
16.8+	Right on John Fountain Road
17.8	Right on NY 9N north
22.7	Left with NY 9N entering Ausable Forks (30.6 on long ride)
	27-mile ride
12.3	Right on Sheldrake Road/Essex 65
14.9	Left across 1-lane bridge
14.9+	Straight onto NY 9N north in Ausable Forks (30.6 on long ride)
	13-mile ride
6.2+	Right across bridge
6.3	Right on Lower Road (no sign) across bridge
6.6	Right on NY 9N north
11.2	Pass under US 87 (41.5 on long ride)

18. KEESEVILLE–JAY

0		2		4 mi
0	2		4 km	

N

sorts lined the river, which literally powered this growth. Keeseville today has very little industry, but remnants of the once mighty mills along the river remain.

This tour starts out easily enough (well, after the short steep grade out of town) and remains so for the shortest ride, but in Clintonville the longer loops climb away from the river and enter a sharply rolling landscape. I find the views on this segment exceptional, well worth the effort required to experience them. You can cross the river to the road home at Ausable Forks, Jay, or Upper Jay. All the loops use NY 9N for the return journey, which can have some traffic and the shoulder width varies, but is almost always rideable. This road is signed as a state bike route and from Upper Jay it follows the East Branch of the Ausable River to Ausable Forks, where the West Branch joins. You are never far from the river and are often riding right next to it. The terrain becomes a bit more rolling from Clintonville to Keeseville, but nowhere does it approach what you experienced on the outbound leg of the ride. Since you're on the same road virtually all the way back, there's little need to refer to the cues and you can simply use the I-87 interchange as a signal to look for Ausable Street, your turnoff for Keeseville, in half a mile.

43-MILE RIDE

0.0 Ride south on US 9/Front Street up the hill.

0.9 Turn right on Augur Lake Road/Essex 15.

1.6 Turn right on Dugway Road. The next few miles have sharp corners and blind crests, so stay to the right and watch for cars.

5.6 Bear right with Dugway Road for some delightful riverside riding.

6.2 Turn left uphill on Green Street.
For 13-mile ride: *Turn right on Dugway Road and continue with cues below.*

9.8 Straight on Green Street where Grove Road is on the right signed for Ausable Forks.

11.0 There is a large exposed rock face on the low mountain to the right.

12.2 Turn left on North Jay Road where Stickney Bridge Road turns right.

I have always enjoyed the great view here, with a small farm in front of you and mountains around the horizon.

For 27-mile ride: *Turn right on Stickney Bridge Road and continue with cues below.*

13.9 Fast downhill into a farming valley with mountains in front of you.

16.8 Turn left on Glen Road/Essex 22 at the bridge in Jay (good pools for swimming here).

The historic Jay covered bridge, erected in 1857, lies on supports next to the road. A nearby sign indicates that a rehabilitation project will restore it for future use.

For 35-mile ride: *Turn right across the one-lane bridge in Jay and continue with cues below.*

17.4 Turn right on Valley Road/Essex 58.

There's a pleasant view after the turn here, with a stream meandering through a meadow and the Brookside farm barn along the road.

20.2 Turn right on Trumbull Corners Road/Essex 12 at a T-intersection.

21.0 Turn right on NY 9N north/Essex 12 in Upper Jay at a T-intersection.

21.1 Turn right with NY 9N where Essex 12 turns left.

24.8 Straight on NY 9N where Essex 86 is left in Jay.

There is a small park here with a gazebo and benches if you want a break.

30.6 Turn left with NY 9N entering Ausable Forks.

30.9 Turn right with NY 9N in Ausable Forks.

36.8 Clintonville.

41.5 Pass under US 87 approaching Keeseville.

42.2 Turn right on Ausable Street.

42.7 **Option:** cross the pedestrian bridge to the start—grated surface, so walk your bike.

42.8 Turn right on Main Street.

Delightful riding on Dugway Road along the Ausable River near Clintonville

42.9 Turn right on Front Street/US 9 S at the flasher.

43.0 Keeseville—end of the tour.

35-MILE RIDE

16.8+ Turn right on John Fountain Road.

17.8 Turn right on NY 9N north at a T-intersection.

22.7 Turn left with NY 9N entering Ausable Forks.
This is mile 30.6 on the long ride.

27-MILE RIDE

12.3 Turn right on Sheldrake Road/Essex 65.

13.4 There is a good view to the left if you're going slowly enough to appreciate it.

14.9 Turn left across the single-lane bridge.

14.9+ Ride straight onto NY 9N north in Ausable Forks.

This is mile 30.6 on the long ride.

13-MILE RIDE

6.2+ Turn right across the bridge.

6.3 Turn right on Lower Road (no sign) on the far side of the bridge.

6.6 Turn right on NY 9N north at a T-intersection.

11.2 Pass under US 87 approaching Keeseville.

This is mile 41.5 on the long ride.

19

Essex–Whallonsburg

*Mountain views, lake views,
and ravishing, rolling roads*

- **DISTANCE:** 25 or 35 miles.

- **TERRAIN/DIFFICULTY:** Lightly to moderately rolling; moderate.

- **START:** Essex, NY, public parking lot across NY 22 from the ferry landing.

- **GETTING THERE/PARKING:** From the north: I-87 to Exit 33 then NY 22 south to Essex; from the south, I-87 to exit 31 then NY 9N east to Westport, north on NY 22 for a brief ways to Essex County 9/Lake Shore Road north to Essex. There are restrooms behind the town office at the main intersection.

There is a wealth of excellent riding on quiet county roads between Lake Champlain and the Adirondacks in the area of Essex. These routes don't exhaust all the possibilities, especially if you don't mind some dirt mixed with your asphalt, but represent the very best of what the area has to offer. Although I find each loop a delight in its entirety, the last 5 miles of this tour are among the most glorious cycling that I've done anywhere.

While in Essex I highly recommend a walking tour of the town (free booklet at the town office). Next to the parking area is the handsome Belden Noble Library, built of stone with balconies on the upper floors facing the lake. On the other side of the library is a large and handsome house, no doubt built by a local captain or shipping magnate.

Leaving the village, you gradually climb up from lake level, with a short steeper pitch just before Middle Road; this is the steepest climb of the entire tour. Middle Road is a beautiful cycling road through open farmland with views on both sides. You turn southwest as you approach the town of Willsboro and the terrain gradually becomes

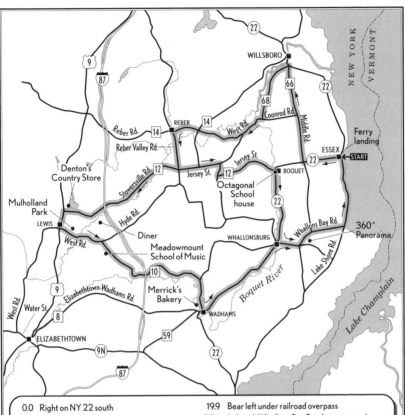

0.0	Right on NY 22 south
0.0+	Right with NY 22 at flasher
1.5	Right on Middle Road/Essex 66 (sign after turn)
5.0	Left on West Road/Essex 68 (no sign) at sign for Stafford
7.3	Right on Coonrod Road
8.3	Right on West Road-Sanders Road bears left
10.1	Straight for Reber with Essex 14
11.2	Left on Reber Valley Road/Essex 57
12.6	Left on Jersey Street/Essex 12 east
	35-mile ride: Right on Stowersville Road/ Essex 12-signed for Lewis (see cues below)
14.1	Right with Jersey St./Essex 12
14.6	Left with Jersey St./Essex 12 signed for Essex
16.8	Sharp S-curve (use caution)
16.9	Left across bridge with Jersey St./Essex 12
17.1	Right on NY 22 south-Essex 12 ends
19.7	Left on Whallons Bay Road in Whallonsburg

19.9	Bear left under railroad overpass
20.6	Left with Whallons Bay Road at crossroads
21.3	Right with Whallons Bay Road at Middle Road
21.7	Trees on downhill create a viewsight for Camel's Hump
22.6	Left on Lake Shore Road at lakefront
25.3+	Left into Essex parking lot
	35-mile ride
17.6	Left on US 9 south in Lewis-signed for Elizabethtown
18.2	Left on West Road/Essex 10 east
20.0	Right on Lewis Road/Essex 10 (no sign)
25.9	Left on NY 22 north in Wadhams
29.8	Right on Whallons Bay Road (sign after turn) in Whallonsburg
30.0	Right under railroad overpass
	This is mile 19.9 on 25-mile ride. Use those cues, adding 10.1 miles.

19. ESSEX–WHALLONSBURG

more rolling, but the climbs are never long or steep and the downhills are joyous. The short loop leaves to return via Boquet and Whallonsburg (note: there are no stores on the short loop), while the long ride continues west to Lewis before turning around. There is an option to extend the long loop from Lewis, which is discussed in the cues. Both loops enjoy a splendid panoramic view of the region shortly after Whallonsburg and then have a great downhill right to the lakeshore, ending with 3 miles of riding along the lake.

Note that these loops can easily be combined with those of tour 6 by taking the Essex–Charlotte ferry. Doing this would provide an all-day ride of 40–77 miles, with excellent scenery on both sides of the lake.

0.0 Turn right on NY 22 south.

0.0+ Turn right with NY 22 at the flasher.

1.5 Turn right on Middle Road/Essex 66 (sign after turn).

3.6 There's a mothballed fleet of old tractors in a field on the left. I counted close to 20 on the property, so this fellow must be a serious collector.

5.0 Turn left on West Road/Essex 68 (no sign) at a sign for Stafford.

7.3 Turn right on Coonrod Road at a T-intersection.

8.3 Bear right on West Road where Sanders Road bears left.

9.5 Cross a new-looking but completely rusted bridge.
This is built of CorTen steel, which strengthens while oxidizing.

10.1 Continue straight for Reber with Essex 14.

10.9 There is a wonderful garden at a house on the right.

11.2 Turn left on Reber Valley Road/Essex 57 at a T-intersection.

12.6 Turn left on Jersey Street/Essex 12 east—signed for Lewis.
For 35-mile ride: *Turn right on Stowersville Road/Essex 12—signed for Lewis and continue at cues below.*
   Option: *From the rise just after a right turn at this intersection there is a view of Camel's Hump, Mount Mansfield, and St. Albans.*

14.1 Turn right with Jersey Street/Essex 12.

14.6 Turn left with Jersey Street/Essex 12 signed for Essex. There are sections of rough pavement ahead, so control your speed and watch the road carefully.

16.8 Caution—sharp S-curves on the downhill and rough pavement.

16.9 Turn left across the bridge with Jersey Street/Essex 12.

17.1 Turn right on NY 22 south where Essex 12 ends.
Across the intersection at the turn is the Boquet octagonal schoolhouse.

18.6 There is a house on the left with an unusual zigzag pattern in the brick used on the front.

19.7 Turn left on Whallons Bay Road in Whallonsburg.

19.9 Bear left under the railroad overpass.

20.6 Turn left with Whallons Bay Road at the crossroads.

20.8 There is a great 360-degree panorama from this location, well worth stopping and dismounting for.
Just after this location, note the birdhouses built at regular intervals on the top of fence posts to the right.

21.3 Bear right with Whallons Bay Road at Middle Road.

21.7 Trees on the downhill create a viewsight for Camel's Hump.

22.6 Turn left on Lake Shore Road at the lakefront.
The peninsula that you see jutting into the lake on the right at this turn is Split Rock, which forms a narrow point in the lake with Thompson Point across from it on the Vermont shore. This rock was often specified in treaties as a dividing line between warring factions and some sources indicate the rock marked the boundary between the tribes of the St. Lawrence and those of the Mohawk Valley. The Treaty of Utrecht, which ended Queen Anne's War in 1713, established Split Rock as the boundary between New France and New England, although France never accepted this.

25.3 Straight at the flasher in Essex.

25.3+ Turn left into the Essex public parking lot—end of the tour.

Unique octagonal stone (former) schoolhouse in Boquet

35-MILE RIDE

16.4 If you're interested in a sit-down lunch, there's a diner at the truck stop on the left.

17.6 Turn left on US 9 south in Lewis—signed for Elizabethtown.

Denton's Country Store is on the right at this corner. If you want to pick up a lunch to go, there's a great place to eat it in a mile; however, use the restroom here.

18.2 Turn left on West Road/Essex 10 east.

Option: *If you wish to extend this ride, you could turn right here on Essex 10 west for Elizabethtown and then take Essex 8 back to Wadhams, which will add about 5 rolling miles. The extra riding will be somewhat more challenging than the basic loop, although not difficult.*

18.6 Mulholland Park is on the left. This is an idyllic spot for lunch or just a break from riding with picnic tables in a wooded area along a stream. However, stopping here does require the sacrifice of braking on a downhill!

20.0 Turn right on Lewis Road/Essex 10 (no sign).

20.4 Meadowmount School of Music is on the right.

This summer music camp was founded in 1944 and offers a seven-week program start-ing in late June for aspiring professional string players and pianists. One imagines that the isolation encourages the students to focus on their music.

24.7 Continue on Essex 10 east where Essex 55 is left.

Shortly after this there's some really pretty riding with the Boquet River on your right and rocky cliffs on the left.

25.9 Turn left on NY 22 north in the small village of Wadhams.

Just before the turn, Merrick's Bakery on the right has excellent coffee (including espresso) and fresh bread. If you go right a short ways you will see the dam and old mill buildings, where a small hydroelectric facility still serves the community.

29.1 A magnificent brick structure complex is on the left.

This is the Essex County Home and Farm, also known as the Whallonsburg County Home and Infirmary, which is on the National Register of Historic Places.

29.8 Bear right on Whallons Bay Road (sign after turn) in Whallonsburg. Ignore the BRIDGE CLOSED sign—there is a pedestrian lane open.

30.0 Turn right under the railroad overpass.

This is mile 19.9 on the 25-mile ride. Use those cues from here and add 10.1 miles to them.

20

Westport Loops

Along the lake and into the hills

- **DISTANCE:** 12 or 23 Miles.
- **TERRAIN/DIFFICULTY:** Generally lightly rolling on the short loop while the long ride is more moderately rolling with a long but gradual climb out of Westport; easy for the short and moderate for the long.
- **START:** Westport—Inn on the Library Lawn at the junction of NY 9N S/NY 22 and Essex County 44/Stevenson Road.
- **GETTING THERE/PARKING:** I-87 to Exit 31 then NY 9N east to Westport. Plenty of parking in the center of town.

Although short, the southern loop on this tour offers pleasant and relatively easy riding with good lake views. The northern loop involves a 4-mile climb out of Westport, so I recommend doing the southern loop first to warm up. This climb shouldn't discourage you, as it is never steep and does have some breaks. Westport is a small town, but has a lively summer tourist season with a number of inns, B&Bs and a theater. Amtrak's daily "Adirondack" also makes a stop here. The southern loop has generally light traffic and would be a good ride for a family. The scenery on this loop is gorgeous on a sunny evening, but, depending on when you ride, Essex 44 will be largely in the shade so you might want to bring an extra layer for warmth.

0.0 Ride south on NY 9N/NY 22 south.

0.9 There is an impressive private, stone arch bridge on the left.

1.0 Turn left on Dudley Road.

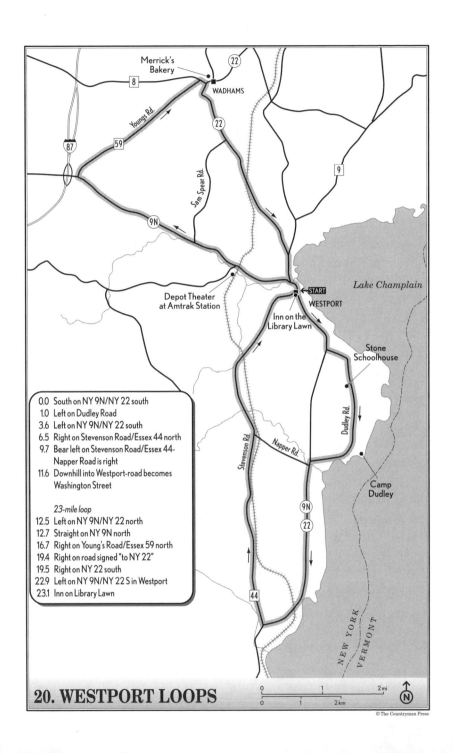

Merrick's Bakery

8

22

WADHAMS

Youngs Rd.

59

22

87

Sam Spear Rd.

9N

9

Lake Champlain

Depot Theater
at Amtrak Station

START
WESTPORT

Inn on the
Library Lawn

Stone
Schoolhouse

Dudley Rd.

Stevenson Rd.

Napper Rd.

9N
22

Camp
Dudley

0.0 South on NY 9N/NY 22 south
1.0 Left on Dudley Road
3.6 Left on NY 9N/NY 22 south
6.5 Right on Stevenson Road/Essex 44 north
9.7 Bear left on Stevenson Road/Essex 44-
    Napper Road is right
11.6 Downhill into Westport-road becomes
    Washington Street

    23-mile loop
12.5 Left on NY 9N/NY 22 north
12.7 Straight on NY 9N north
16.7 Right on Young's Road/Essex 59 north
19.4 Right on road signed "to NY 22"
19.5 Right on NY 22 south
22.9 Left on NY 9N/NY 22 S in Westport
23.1 Inn on Library Lawn

44

NEW YORK

VERMONT

0   1   2 mi
0   1   2 km

N

20. WESTPORT LOOPS

Trio of cyclists on a quiet road

1.8 There is a tiny, one-room brick schoolhouse on the right, built in 1816 and used for exactly a century.

2.9 Camp Dudley, on the left, is the oldest boys camp in continuous operation (since 1885) in the country. From my observations while riding by, they now also accept girl campers.

3.6 Turn left on NY 9N/NY 22 south at a T-intersection.

4.5 There is an excellent view from here of the Green Mountains across the lake.

5.8 Drop down to lake level.

5.9 Caution—there is a very narrow shoulder with a ditch on the right here.

6.3 You have a view of Crown Point Bridge down the lake, but it is easiest to spot with late-afternoon sunlight glancing off it.

6.5 Turn right on Stevenson Road/Essex 44 north—be careful of loose sand at this sharp turn.

7.9 If you want some very cool and fresh water, there is a pipe on the left from a nearby spring.

9.7 Bear left on Stevenson Road/Essex 44 where Napper Road is right.

11.0 Caution—cross a RR track at a sharp angle.

11.6 Start of the downhill into Westport; this road becomes Washington Street.

12.5 Inn on the library Lawn—end of the southern loop.

23-MILE LOOP

12.5 Turn left on NY 9N/NY 22 north.

12.6 Westport Federated Church has a unique and interesting steeple.

12.7 Continue straight on NY 9N north.

13.6 The Westport Depot Theatre is in the old train station on the left—the Amtrak Adirondack still stops here daily.

16.7 Turn right on Young's Road/Essex 59 north.

19.4 Turn right on the road signed "to NY 22".

19.5 Turn right on NY 22 south at a T-intersection.
You can optionally turn left to explore the small village of Wadhams. Merrick's Bakery is around the corner to the left after crossing the Boquet River and has excellent coffee, including espresso, cappuccino, and the like.

21.3 Caution—you cross a RR track at a sharp angle.

22.9 Turn left on NY 9N/NY 22 south in Westport.

23.1 Inn on the Library Lawn—end of the tour.

TICONDEROGA AND THE NEW YORK SOUTHERN TOURS

The view looking north from Mount Defiance

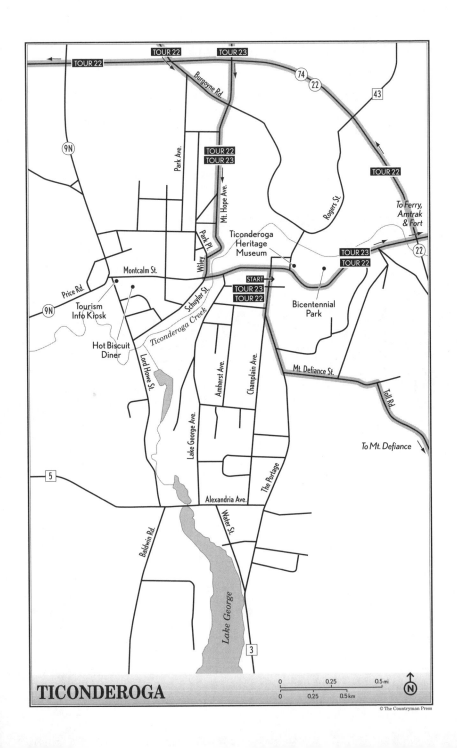

TOUR 22

TOUR 22   TOUR 23

Burgoyne Rd.

74
22

43

TOUR 22

Park Ave.

TOUR 22
TOUR 23

Mt. Hope Ave.

Rogers St.

To Ferry,
Amtrak
& Fort

9N

Park Pl.

Wiley

Ticonderoga
Heritage
Museum

TOUR 23
TOUR 22

22

Montcalm St.

Price Rd.

Schuyler St.

START
TOUR 23
TOUR 22

Bicentennial
Park

9N

Tourism
Info Kiosk

Ticonderoga Creek

Hot Biscuit
Diner

Mt. Defiance St.

Toll Rd.

Lord Howe St.

Amherst Ave.

Champlain Ave.

To Mt. Defiance

Lake George Ave.

The Portage

5

Alexandria Ave.

Water St.

Baldwin Rd.

Lake George

3

TICONDEROGA

0   0.25   0.5 mi

0   0.25   0.5 km

N

© The Countryman Press

EVERYONE ASSOCIATES THE TOWN OF TICONDEROGA with the famed fort, although most people don't know the details of the fort's history. The French first guarded the New York shore at this narrow point in the lake in 1755 with Fort Carillon. In 1758 they successfully defended their fort against a far larger British force, but lost the return engagement a year later. In the early morning of May 10, 1775, just weeks after the battles at Lexington and Concord, Ethan Allen and Benedict Arnold surprised a small British garrison that was not aware hostilities had broken out. The following winter Henry Knox and his men hauled the fort's cannons to Boston where they were used to force the British to withdraw to Halifax on March 26, 1776.

In the summer of 1777 a large British force under General Burgoyne worked its way down Lake Champlain, certain of victory. Rather than attack Fort Ticonderoga directly, they hauled their cannon up nearby Mount Defiance, which had a commanding position over the fort that the Americans had failed to defend. Immediately realizing the futility of holding the fort, the defenders withdrew under cover of night. That fall General Burgoyne was defeated and surrendered his troops at Saratoga, changing the ultimate course of the war.

Ticonderoga is just a few miles from the northern end of Lake George, a major summer recreation destination and generally not a good area for cycling due to the crowded roads. The Ticonderoga Heritage Museum, located in a building that used to be the main office of a large paper mill in downtown Ticonderoga, is open weekends from Memorial Day to Columbus Day and daily from July 1 through Labor Day. The museum contains a number of exhibits on local history and industry and is also the starting point for several walking tours in Ticonderoga.

There is a cluster of motels near the circle where NY 9N meets Montcalm Avenue, which is also the location of a small seasonal tourism info booth. There is a range of dining options in town and nearby.

Tourism Info

Ticonderoga Area Chamber of Commerce, 94 Montcalm Street (518-585-6619 or www.ticonderogany.com)

Bike Shops

There are no bike shops in Ticonderoga and the nearest ones are in Glens Falls, Lake Placid, or Middlebury, so make certain that your bike is in good condition before starting any of the rides in this region.

MOUNT DEFIANCE OPTION

This information is included here as all the tours starting in or passing through Ticonderoga have access to this option. Mount Defiance provides an excellent view of the region at the expense of a very steep 1-mile climb on a narrow and twisting road. The view is particularly impressive in the late afternoon and evening, when the setting sun illuminates the Vermont farmland spread out in front of you across the lake. The very best views are in the hour or two before sunset (on a clear day, obviously), so if you're overnighting in Ti this is a highly recommended evening activity. You could also lock your bike near the gate and walk up the road if that is more palatable. The access gate is usually locked to automobile traffic at around 5–6 PM, so if the gate is locked that means you will have the road all to yourself.

Mount Defiance played an important role in American history. While the Revolutionary army occupied the fort, they believed Mount Defiance too steep to scale and therefore didn't feel compelled to station troops there. However, General Burgoyne reclaimed Fort Ticonderoga for the British simply by ordering cannon into position on its summit and trained on the fort in July of 1777. The Americans, recognizing their position as untenable, quietly withdrew overnight rather than be bombarded from the commanding position Mount Defiance provided the British.

These cues start at the intersection of Montcalm Street (the main drag in Ticonderoga) and Champlain Avenue.

0.0 Ride south (uphill) on Champlain Avenue from Montcalm Street (this is as downtown as Ticonderoga gets).

0.1 Bear left onto The Portage. (Named after the nearby Native American canoe portage route to Lake George.)

0.3 Turn left on Mount Defiance Street at the sign for the mountain.

0.5 Ignore the DEAD END sign (well, OK—it's technically true, but you don't care).

0.7 Turn right uphill on the Toll Road (perhaps in former times, but now in name only).

1.7 Summit with spectacular views of the lake, fort, and surrounding region.
Note: You'll need to brake a lot on the descent, but feather the brakes on and off repeatedly instead of clamping down on them continuously and causing a dangerous heat buildup. Stop to rest yourself and your brakes if you need to.

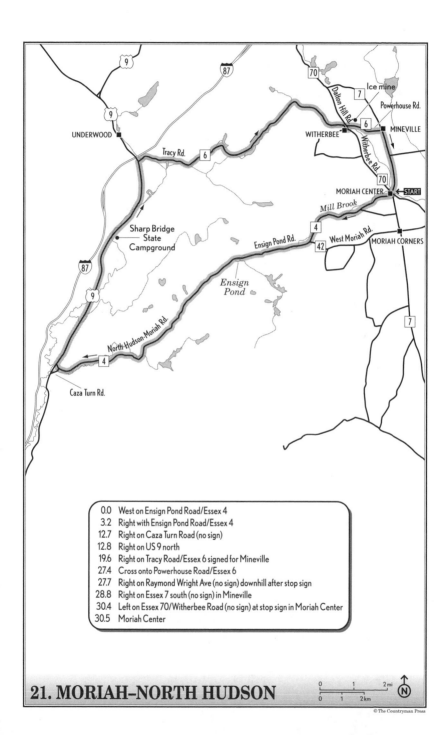

0.0	West on Ensign Pond Road/Essex 4
3.2	Right with Ensign Pond Road/Essex 4
12.7	Right on Caza Turn Road (no sign)
12.8	Right on US 9 north
19.6	Right on Tracy Road/Essex 6 signed for Mineville
27.4	Cross onto Powerhouse Road/Essex 6
27.7	Right on Raymond Wright Ave (no sign) downhill after stop sign
28.8	Right on Essex 7 south (no sign) in Mineville
30.4	Left on Essex 70/Witherbee Road (no sign) at stop sign in Moriah Center
30.5	Moriah Center

21. MORIAH–NORTH HUDSON

0   1   2 mi
0   1   2 km

N

© The Countryman Press

Moriah–North Hudson

Quiet remote roads and a cool finish

- **DISTANCE:** 31 miles
- **TERRAIN/DIFICULTY:** Lightly to moderately rolling; moderate.
- **START:** Intersection of Essex 7 and Essex 4/Ensign Pond Road in Moriah Center.
- **GETTING THERE/PARKING:** I-87 to Exit 30, then Essex 6/Tracy Road east, then Essex 70 south in Witherbee to Moriah Center. You will need to check locally for parking as there are no public parking areas here. I asked at the Ironville Oil Company and was told that cyclists could park out of the way in the back, although you should always check first so they know who the car belongs to and how long it will be there.

This tour spends most of its time on remote, lightly traveled, twisting backcountry roads. How remote? The only stores on this ride are in a 2-mile stretch at the start/end. How lightly traveled? On Essex County routes 4 and 6 you might see one car for every mile you ride. How twisting? On these same roads, if there are any tangential sections at all they are less than a football field long.

Essex County 6 is a delightful road that I knew cyclists would love as soon as I saw it, and when I discovered Essex County 4, I knew these roads would form a great loop. Both roads climb gradually along watercourses, then have gently rolling terrain where they cross watersheds, finally descending along another stream. These isolated roads are connected by US 9, which is almost as traffic-free due to the parallel Northway. This tour is not for those seeking spectacular scenery or lake views, but it does provide very enjoyable riding through Adirondack woodlands. It would be a good choice for a hot day, as you are in shade much of the time. There are two trailheads on Essex 4 with hikes of less than a mile if that appeals to you.

This area was a major iron ore–mining center starting about 1825 and continuing through World War II. There were said to be some 20 sawmills on Mill Brook between Ensign Pond (about mile 5 on your route) and the lake in the first half of the 19th century. Lumber was rafted to Canada from the dock in Port Henry early in the century and to southern markets after the Champlain Canal opened in 1823; iron ore was also shipped out by boat. When the railroad was completed along the west shore of the lake, the Lake Champlain & Moriah branch line was built for bringing the ore down the mountain for transfer to the main line or local smelters at Port Henry. Before this ox teams were used on a plank road, which is noted by a historical marker in Mineville. The major mines were located in Mineville and Witherbee; these were company towns and you can still see the rows of company houses constructed with blocks made from iron ore tailings. Those interested in this region's industrial heritage can visit the Iron Center museum in Port Henry.

0.0 Ride west on Ensign Pond Road/Essex 4.

This road can be hard to spot as it leaves Essex 7 right next to a building and the sign is hidden from the north side. You will start climbing almost immediately and the grade out of Moriah Center is the steepest you will encounter on the entire tour.

3.2 Turn right with Ensign Pond Road/Essex 4 where Windy Hill Road/Essex 42 joins from the left.

After another mile of gradual climbing, you pass through a delightful area with moss-covered rock faces to the left and a gurgling stream below you on the right. A half-mile farther you pass some beaver dams controlling the flow of the stream. Shortly after this you gain the height of land and ride through an expansive marshy area with Ensign Pond on the left. This is a great place to stop and enjoy the solitude and placid natural surroundings.

7.5 On the left is a carved stone road marker from 1870, identifying the Port Henry–Moriah–North Hudson state road.

12.7 Turn right on Caza Turn Road (no sign) at a T-intersection.

12.8 Turn right on US 9 north at a T-intersection.

Seriously twisting Essex County 4

This road is paved with old concrete here, which has fairly large gaps between the sections, but it gratefully turns to asphalt shortly.

17.1 Sharp Bridge State Campground is on the right.

There may be a small day-use fee for entry. This is a great place for lunch or a break in your ride, with covered picnic tables, restrooms and some interesting benches carved out of thick logs.

19.6 Turn right on Tracy Road/Essex 6 signed for Mineville.

This road is similar to Essex 4, but it seems even more twisting with somewhat less climbing.

27.4 Cross Witherbee/Dalton Hill Roads onto Powerhouse Road/Essex 6.

You'll feel the temperature drop by 10–15 degrees as you pass an ice mine at the fenced-in area on the left.

This is an old mine shaft that's been flooded and most of the water is permanently frozen. The family living across the street says they stay cool on even the hottest days.

27.7 Bear right on Raymond Wright Avenue (no sign) downhill after the stop sign.

28.8 Turn right on Essex 7 south (no sign) in Mineville, and keep your hands near the brake levers.

There is a sign for Moriah Shock to the left, which is an incarceration facility for young offenders that tries to "scare them straight"; the shocks are not electric but psychological.

There is a historical marker for the old plank road in front of the cemetery.

30.4 Turn left on Essex 70/Witherbee Road (no sign) at the stop sign in Moriah Center.

30.5 Moriah Center—end of the tour.

22

Ticonderoga–Ironville

Some climbing, a little history, and then a descent

- **DISTANCE:** 23 miles
- **TERRAIN/DIFFICULTY:** Moderately rolling—the ride begins with a long, gradual climb, then level and mostly downhill riding; moderate.
- **START:** Intersection of Montcalm Street and Champlain Avenue in downtown Ticonderoga.
- **GETTING THERE/PARKING:** I-87 to Exit 28, New York 74 east for 19 miles to Ticonderoga. Plentiful free parking is available in town.

Like some loans, this ride is "front-end loaded." The vast majority of the climbing is done in the first 5 miles, after which you are more than amply rewarded with some lovely lakeside riding, a historical museum in a tiny hamlet, and exhilarating downhills. I rode this early on a summer morning, before I even had breakfast, and found it a most glorious and satisfying way to start the day. After the initial climbing, there is 3 miles of bucolic, lightly rolling riding that brings you to the historic hamlet of Ironville and the Penfield Museum. You then enjoy 4 miles of downhill to Crown Point, with rolling terrain and more downhills bringing you back to Ti.

0.0 Ride east on Montcalm Street (downhill).

0.1 The Ticonderoga Heritage Museum is on the left.

Bicentennial Park behind the museum was once occupied by a sprawling International Paper facility, until it moved several miles north in 1968. The museum is housed in the only surviving structure from the complex, which had been the main offices. A marker across the street from the museum marks the landing for "The Great Carry," the Native American canoe portage between Lake Champlain and Lake George.

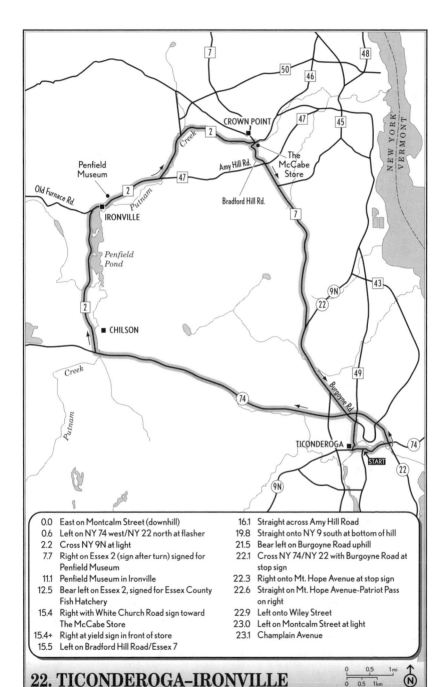

0.0	East on Montcalm Street (downhill)
0.6	Left on NY 74 west/NY 22 north at flasher
2.2	Cross NY 9N at light
7.7	Right on Essex 2 (sign after turn) signed for Penfield Museum
11.1	Penfield Museum in Ironville
12.5	Bear left on Essex 2, signed for Essex County Fish Hatchery
15.4	Right with White Church Road sign toward The McCabe Store
15.4+	Right at yield sign in front of store
15.5	Left on Bradford Hill Road/Essex 7
16.1	Straight across Amy Hill Road
19.8	Straight onto NY 9 south at bottom of hill
21.5	Bear left on Burgoyne Road uphill
22.1	Cross NY 74/NY 22 with Burgoyne Road at stop sign
22.3	Right onto Mt. Hope Avenue at stop sign
22.6	Straight on Mt. Hope Avenue-Patriot Pass on right
22.9	Left onto Wiley Street
23.0	Left on Montcalm Street at light
23.1	Champlain Avenue

22. TICONDEROGA–IRONVILLE

0.6 Turn left on NY 74 west/NY 22 north at the flasher.

2.2 Cross NY 9N at the light.

3.1 You can see the road rising in front of you as a climbing lane begins.
Although the climb is 2 miles long, the gradient is a manageable 7 percent or so. With the climbing lane and shoulder you can ride as slowly as you need to without worrying about traffic.

5.2 You've reached the top of the main climb, but there is still an easy dip and low rise remaining.

7.2 The shoulder narrows, but you'll be getting off this road soon.

7.7 Turn right on Essex 2 (sign after turn) signed for the Penfield Museum.
This road initially borders a marshland along Putnam Creek, but then dives into cool woods in a series of twists and turns, mixed with ever so slight rises and drops. You then emerge along Penfield Pond before entering the village of Ironville.

11.1 The Penfield Museum is on your left, housed in a large and handsome house, as you enter the hamlet of Ironville, where all the structures are painted a classic white.
The museum is open from May 15 to October 15, 10–4, with a noon opening on Sunday; admission fee. Besides the customary local historical artifacts and period rooms, the museum exhibits a large electromagnet, claimed to be the beginning of the electrical age. The magnet was made by Joseph Henry of Albany and used locally in the extraction of iron from raw ore, increasingly in demand for the new railroads of the time; this was the first documented use of electricity in industry. The magnet was later sold to Thomas Davenport of Brandon, Vermont, who went on to create and receive a patent for the first electrical motor.

Leaving the museum, continue straight on the road you had been on, Essex 2. You will soon start a downhill that lasts the better part of the next 4 miles.

12.5 Bear left on Essex 2, signed for Essex County Fish Hatchery, where Amy Hill Road continues straight over Putnam Creek.
You follow Putnam Creek for the next 2 miles, with intermittent falls and possible swimming holes.

14.8 There is an attractive section here where the stream drops over a series of ledges, but you might be going too fast to appreciate it.

The Penfield Museum in Ironville, birthplace of the electrical age

15.3 If you're not already, start serious braking where you see a crossroads sign.

15.4 Turn right with the sign for White Church Road toward The McCabe Store, a classic country store that can provide food or cooling beverages.

15.4+ Turn right at the yield sign directly in front of the store.

15.5 Turn left on Bradford Hill Road/Essex 7—be ready for sharp turns with limited vision and a steep climb over the next half-mile.
There is the stone skeleton of an old mill in the woods near this turn. A short path leads from a dirt parking area.

16.1 Ride straight across Amy Hill Road.
The next 2 miles are moderately rolling, after which you will have level and mostly downhill riding.

19.3 There is a brief view of the lake to the left, with the white plumes from the paper mill dominating the scene.

19.8 Ride straight onto NY 9 N south at the bottom of the hill.

21.5 Bear left on Burgoyne Road uphill.

22.1 Cross NY 74/ NY 22 with Burgoyne Road at a stop sign.

22.3 Turn right onto Mount Hope Avenue at a stop sign.

22.6 Stay straight on Mount Hope Avenue where Patriot Pass is on the right.

22.9 Turn left at a T-intersection onto Wiley Street.

23.0 Turn left on Montcalm Street at the light.

23.1 Champlain Avenue—end of the tour.

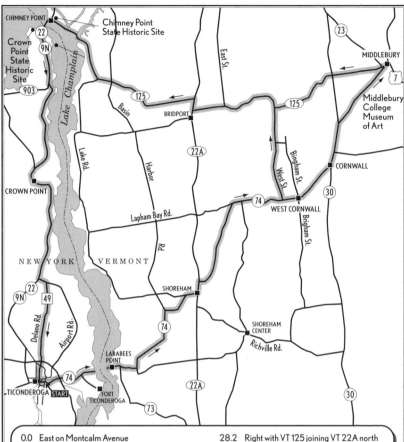

0.0	East on Montcalm Avenue
0.6	Cross NY 22 onto NY 74 east at flasher.
1.1	Fort Road, entrance to Fort Ticonderoga, on right
2.1	Ticonderoga ferry landing
2.2	Ride on VT 74 east from Larabees Point ferry landing
2.6	Straight on VT 74 at VT 73
7.1	Right with VT 74 entering Shoreham
7.5	Left with VT 74 joining VT 22A north
7.9	Right with VT 74
	For 43-mile ride: Left on West Street-3.4 miles to main route by continuing straight on VT 125 west (mile 24.6)-subtract 8 miles from remaining cues
15.6	Left on VT 30 north
17.0	Right with VT 30
19.8	Sharp left on VT 125 at sign for College St.
24.6	Right with VT 125
28.2	Right with VT 125 joining VT 22A north in Bridport
28.7	Left with VT 125
35.9	Straight across Chimney Point bridge
38.5	Left on Lake Road/Essex 48
39.8	Left with Lake Road after crossing track
42.0	Left on NY 9N/NY 22 south
42.6	Left with NY 9N/NY 22 in Crown Point
46.8	Left on Shore Airport Road
47.1	Right on Delano Road/Essex 49
50.1	Cross NY 74 onto Mt. Hope Avenue
50.5	Straight on Mt. Hope Avenue-Patriot Pass bears right
50.8	Left on Wiley Street
50.9	Left on Montcalm Street at light
51.1	Champlain Avenue

23. TICONDEROGA–CHIMNEY POINT

0   1   2 mi
0   1   2 km

Ticonderoga–Chimney Point

A college, a bridge, and two forts

- **DISTANCE:** 51 or 43 miles.
- **TERRAIN/DIFFICULTY:** Lightly to moderately rolling; moderate.
- **START:** Intersection of Montcalm Street and Champlain Avenue in downtown Ticonderoga.
- **GETTING THERE/PARKING:** I-87 to Exit 28, New York 74 east for 19 miles to Ticonderoga. Plentiful free parking is available in town.

This tour provides a very scenic ride with the opportunity to explore the attractive and interesting college town of Middlebury, and possibly have a relaxed lunch there in one of its fine restaurants. Unless you're the sort of rider who doesn't like to stop for more than a few minutes after warming up, I recommend planning this as an all-day event with an extended stop in Middlebury.

Shortly after leaving Ticonderoga you ride on the historic Ticonderoga ferry, which has been taking people, wagons, animals, cars, and bicycles across the lake for well over two centuries. Once in Vermont the route follows VT 73 on rolling roads to the small town of Shoreham, passing by farms and apple orchards on the way. You continue on VT 73 as it climbs a ridge with views of the Green Mountains and the Adirondacks, then pick up VT 30 in Cornwall and follow it into Middlebury. The 43-mile ride bypasses Middlebury if you decide you don't want to do the longer loop.

There are numerous distractions in Middlebury, including the architecturally rich Middlebury College campus and art museum, or the Frog Hollow State Craft Center, and scores of other attractive shops and places to eat. Leaving Middlebury you ride west on VT 125 with ever-closer views of the Adirondacks as you approach the lake at

Chimney Point. There are optional visits to historic sites on either side of the bridge, the only one spanning the lake in its entire length. Smooth riding on lightly rolling roads brings you back to the start. This tour can be combined with tour 2 to create an extended 2–3 day tour.

0.0 Ride east (downhill) on Montcalm Avenue.

0.1 The Ticonderoga Heritage Museum is on the left.
Bicentennial Park behind the museum was once occupied by a sprawling International Paper facility, until it moved several miles north in 1968. The museum is housed in the only surviving structure from the complex, which had been the main office.

0.6 Cross NY 22 onto NY 74 east at the flasher.

1.1 Fort Road, the entrance to Fort Ticonderoga, is on the right.

2.1 Ticonderoga ferry landing. During the summer season the ferry crosses on a generally continual basis.

2.2 Ride on VT 74 east from the Larabees Point ferry landing.

2.3 On the right are spools of cable for the ferry, which must be replaced every four years. Just past this on the left is a mural painted on the side of a barn.

2.6 Continue straight on VT 74 at VT 73. VT 74 makes a number of 90-degree turns over the next several miles and in all cases follow the main road.
This is farming country and you'll be passing farms and orchards all the way to Shoreham. The road will be rolling and more uphill than down as you climb away from the lake.

7.1 Bear right with VT 74 entering Shoreham.

7.5 Turn left with VT 74 where it joins VT 22A north at a T-intersection.

7.9 Turn right with VT 74.
You will gently climb to the top of a low ridge that offers alternating views of the Green Mountains to the right and the Adirondacks to the left.

13.2 *For 43-mile ride:* Turn left here on West Street, which has wonderful open views toward the lake. It is 3.4 miles to where you rejoin the main route by continuing straight on VT 125 west (mile 24.6); subtract 8 miles from the remaining cues.

A rider on the historic Ticonderoga cable ferry

13.8 Cross Bingham Street in West Cornwall—there are some attractive houses here.

15.6 Turn left on VT 30 north at a T-intersection.

16.8 There is a former stone blacksmith shop on the left.

17.0 Bear right with VT 30.

19.2 The Middlebury College Museum of Art is on the right and should be open during the day.
There is bike parking in front of the building or you should be able to bring your bike into the building if you wish.

19.8 Turn sharply left on VT 125 west at the sign for College Street as you enter downtown Middlebury.
Option: *Continue straight to explore Middlebury or possibly have an early lunch. Middlebury is an enjoyable town with interesting shops and excellent restaurants. Add whatever mileage you accumulate to the following cues.*

24.6 Turn right with VT 125 where West Street (43-mile ride) enters from the left.

28.2 Turn right with VT 125 where it joins VT 22A north in Bridport.

28.7 Turn left with VT 125 and enjoy the view.

33.6 You have your first sight of the elegant Chimney Point Bridge.

34.6 Ride over a tree-lined causeway between the lake and a marsh.
In spring high water, the lake is often lapping at the edge of the road or even flowing over it by a few inches.

35.9 Continue straight across the Chimney Point Bridge.
This area got its name because after the British burned all of the French structures here, the chimneys were all that was left standing. You can optionally visit the museum at the Chimney Point State Historic Site on the left just before the bridge. The museum contains a number of exhibits on the early Native American and French settlers in this area. The museum is open Wednesday through Sunday, 9:30–5 from late May to mid-October (802 759-2412); admission fee. The road crossing the bridge becomes NY 903 on the far side (or is it technically at the middle of the bridge?).

36.5 Just as you come down off the bridge there is a visitors center on the opposite side of the road that has plenty of information and brochures about points of interest in the region.

From the same location the Crown Point fort ruins are to the right—the easiest (certainly shortest) way to reach them is to dismount and walk across the grass. If you continue to the official entrance road you'll find that you've done an extra mile or so of riding due to its circuitous approach. There is a small museum (admission fee) with primarily military exhibits, but it's free to wander around the remains of the ramparts and there is a signed walking tour. Of interest is the fact that the ruins you see represent fortifications built by both the French and the English at different points in the long history of their battle for control of Lake Champlain.

38.5 Turn left on Lake Road/Essex 48. This is a delightfully quiet road for cycling.

39.8 Turn left with Lake Road after crossing the track.

42.0 Caution—Turn left on NY 9N/NY 22 south at a T-intersection at the bottom of a blind downhill curve. There can be moderate traffic on this road.

42.6 Turn left with NY 9N/NY 22 in the small town of Crown Point. There is a store here and a large park just before the turn if you want a break from riding.

46.8 Turn left on Shore Airport Road.

47.1 Turn right on Delano Road/Essex 49, which is a wonderfully rolling farm road.

Although this road has some climbing, I find it far preferable to the boring Shore Airport Road, which passes by the large paper mill that generates the white plume of smoke that you can see. Depending on the wind direction, you may also get some scent from the mill, although I'm told that it's not related to the smoke.

50.1 Cross NY 74 onto Mount Hope Avenue entering Ticonderoga.

50.5 Stay straight on Mount Hope Avenue where Patriot Pass bears right.

50.8 Turn left on Wiley Street at a T-intersection.

50.9 Turn left on Montcalm Street at the light.

51.1 Champlain Avenue—end of the tour.

MULTIPLE-DAY
TOURS

ALTHOUGH I LIKE MANY TYPES of cycling, I particularly enjoy touring. Essentially, this means riding a bike on a trip of two or more consecutive days. I find it especially satisfying to stay in a town or city having cycled there, especially if it is new to me. There are several types of touring, the most popular being fully-supported tours offered by commercial touring companies or sponsored by bicycle clubs. These will have a sag van accompanying the group to carry the luggage between lodging places and also support the cyclists on the road, usually carrying the lunches and perhaps assisting with needed repairs.

Self-supported touring implies that you have no support vehicle and are carrying all the gear that you will need over the duration of the tour. There are a number of specific varieties in this category. Credit card touring is much as it sounds, the phrase implying that you are carrying a piece of plastic and not a whole lot else. You might pack a pair of walking shorts, a shirt and sandals to wear to dinner, but will probably wash out your riding clothes in the evening for the next day's cycling. This style is best suited to a fast-paced, high-mileage weekend trip. Other folks will carry more gear, especially for tours of longer duration or to provide comfort in varying weather conditions. Lastly, there are those who prefer to camp and for the most part cook their own meals, which is sometimes known as fully loaded touring. This rugged breed can often be recognized by the camping gear on their racks or their front and rear panniers, needed to carry all their equipment while balancing the load on the bike.

This book has two trips that are defined as multiple-day tours, but there are several other possibilities for rides covering more than one day, partly depending on your preferred daily distance. Tours 2 and 23 can be combined as a two-day loop with an overnight in Middlebury, or even a three-day tour with the second night spent in Ticonderoga. The latter would be particularly appropriate if you wished to spend extensive time exploring the famed fort and other historic sites in the area. Tour 5 can be done as a two-day excursion, staying in Burlington with its many attractions and diverse, excellent restaurants. Tour 14 can be extended to two days if you prefer a slower pace or fewer miles per day. There are motels both in Quebec and at Rouses Point.

Although tour 24 is described as a two-day weekend trip, you can optionally add a third day by riding to Ticonderoga the second day before returning to Burlington. Tour 25 is described as a nine-day circumnavigation of the entire lake, with an extension to Montreal and a free day there to explore. However, it can be adapted for a tighter schedule or a desire for shorter mileages each day. If at all possible I encourage you to ride all the way around the lake to see and enjoy its many regions, but a shorter excursion can be just as satisfying. Details of the variations are in the tour 25 section.

24

Burlington–Lake Placid (Keene)

The Adirondack Explorer

- **DISTANCE**: 109 miles over two days of riding or 82 miles in one day.
- **TERRAIN/DIFFICULTY**: Lightly rolling to mountainous; challenging.
- **START**: Burlington ferry landing (cues start at the Port Kent ferry landing).
- **GETTING THERE/PARKING**: For Burlington, I-89 to Exit 14, then US 2 west to the lake. There are pay parking lots along the lake, but you may also find free overnight parking on the fringes of downtown. If you spend the prior night at a hotel in Burlington, you can probably leave your car there for two days.

This route is presented as a two-day tour between Burlington and Lake Placid, and with a shorter—but equally difficult—day ride option through Keene and back. Both versions provide excellent riding and stunning scenery, using several of my favorite roads in the eastern Adirondack region. There is an adventurous option on the day ride that involves rough dirt roads (more like jeep tracks); see the cues for details.

The first day has a fairly short mileage, which will give you time to explore Lake Placid. Despite its fame, I must admit that I find it a bit on the tacky side of things. It is beautifully situated and there are some quality shops and good restaurants, but many of the stores pander the typical tourist fare that can be purchased elsewhere, even though embossed with an "Adirondack" or "Lake Placid" label. I recall having breakfast in a restaurant and a friend ordered pancakes, paying extra for Adirondack maple syrup. Sure enough, that was what the label on the front of the small bottle claimed, but on the back was printed the phrase, "Product of Quebec." The second day is substantially longer, but

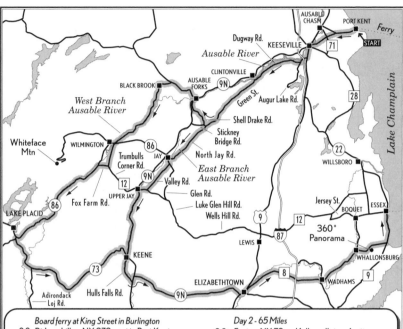

Board ferry at King Street in Burlington

0.0 Ride uphill on NY 373 west in Port Kent
1.8 Bear left on Soper Road/Essex 17
4.3 Right on Kent Street in Keeseville
4.4 Left on US 9/Front Street at flasher
5.5 Right on Augar Lake Road/Essex 15
6.2 Right on Dugway Road
10.1 Right with Dugway Road
10.8 Left uphill on Green Street
16.8 Right on Stickney Bridge Road
82-mile ride: Left on North Jay Road and continue (see cues below)
16.9 Right on Sheldrake Road/Essex 65
19.5 Left across one-lane bridge
19.5+ Straight on US 9N north in AusableForks
19.8 Straight on Golf Course Road-US 9N turns right
19.9 Left on Essex 15/Silver Lake Road signed for Black Brook
20.8 Bear left with Essex 15 signed for Black Brook
22.9 Bear left with Essex 15 signed for Black Brook
23.9 Bear left with Haselton Road (sign after turn) signed for Wilmington
24.0 Left at T-junction onto Black Brook Road (no sign-becomes Essex 12)
30.9 Cross NY 86 with Essex 12 in Wilmington
32.7 Right on Indian Rock Road
33.6 Left onto NY 86
43.7 Junction with NY 73 in Lake Placid

Day 2 - 65 Miles

0.0 East on NY 73 and follow all signs for it
14.4 Right on Halls Falls Road/Essex 69 in Keene after bridge
16.9 Left on NY 73 west (no sign)
17.4 Right on NY 9N south for Elizabethtown
27.7 Left with NY 9N south/US 9 north in Elizabethtown
28.1 Straight on US 9 north
28.3 Right on Essex 8 signed for Wadhams
35.6 Left on Essex 22 in Wadhams
39.5 Right on Whallons Bay Road (sign after turn) in Whallonsburg
39.7 Right under railroad overpass
40.4 Left with Whallons Bay Road at crossroads
41.1 Right with Whallons Bay Road
42.4 Left on Lake Shore Road at lakefront
45.1+ Right into Essex ferry landing
45.2 VT F5 from Charlotte ferry landing
45.6 Right on VT F5 at crossroads
46.6 Left on Lake Road
49.9 Left on Greenbush Road
51.6 Right on Bostwick Road
53.5 Left on US 7
54.8 Right on Webster Road just after bridge
54.9 Right on Webster Road (no sign) at stop sign
56.0 Left on Spear Street

24. BURLINGTON–LAKE PLACID (KEENE)

(See Tour 8 map on page 88 and Burlington map on page 72 for the Vermont portion of this tour.)

(continued from previous page)	*Alternate (avoids bike path)*
59.7 Left on bike path at white barn at Swift Street	59.7 Cross Swift Street at light
60.2 Sharp right downhill on the bike path; cross bridge (dangerous when wet)	61.9 Left on US 2 west/Main Street from "rotary" at UVM campus (hotels/motels to right)
61.0 Right with path at bottom of downhill.	63.6 Left on Battery Street (right for Wyndham)
61.1 Left on Swift Street with path	63.8 King Street ferry landing
61.1+ Right with wider path onto Farrell Street	
61.4 Cross Farrell Street with path then right; turn left at corner	*82-mile ride*
61.7 Cross US 7 at light to Home Avenue	18.4 Fast downhill
62.2 Cross RR tracks to Austin Drive	21.3 Left on Glen Road/Essex 22 at bridge
62.7 Right on path	22.0 Right on Valley Road/Essex 58
62.9 Straight on road bordered by boulders	24.8 Right on Trumbull Corners Road/Essex 12-Essex 58 ends
63.2 Bear left on path-where road curves right	25.5 Left on NY 9N south in Upper Jay
63.5 Right on Harrison Avenue when path ends	31.5 Right on NY 73 west in Keene and left immediately on Hulls Falls Road
63.7 Left on path just before tracks	*This is mile 14.4 on 2nd day of 2-day tour;*
64.9 King Street ferry landing	*add 17.1 miles to those cues for rest of ride.*

much of this is downhill. However, if you have the luxury of doing so, you might plan to spend the second night enjoying the pleasures of Burlington before heading home.

Although this is proposed as a two-day tour, it can easily be extended to three days with the second night spent in Ticonderoga. For that option, see the cues for day 8 of tour 25, which will get you to Ti from Lake Placid. From there, use the cues for tour 23 to get to Middlebury and then day 2 of tour 25 to get back to Burlington. Whether you're doing the basic or extended tour, I strongly recommend reserving your lodging well in advance, especially in the summer or foliage season. It is difficult to get a room for just one night on a weekend in Lake Placid, but I suggest checking with the Lake Placid/Essex County Convention and Visitors Bureau at 216 Main Street (1-800-44PLACID), as they can determine the status of most rooms in town on their system.

On the day-ride option, you continue with seriously rolling terrain to Jay and Upper Jay along the East Branch of the Ausable River, while the two-day tour turns north for Ausable Forks. From Upper Jay you have an easy and gradual climb along the river to Keene, where you rejoin the route from Lake Placid.

Lake Placid Bike Shops

High Peaks Cyclery Mountain Adventure Center, 331 Main Street (518-523-3764; 877-523-3764 or mail@highpeakscyclery.com)

Maui North Ski, Bike and Surf Co., 134 Main Street (518-523-7245 or mauinorth@westel-com.com)

Placid Planet, 51 Saranac Avenue (518-523-4128 or placidpl@adelphia.net)

DAY 1: 44 MILES

From the ferry landing you climb for 2 miles as you leave lake level, but then ride on a plateau before dropping into Keeseville. Leaving town, there is some very pleasant riding on Dugway Road, with a mile along the Ausable River. You then turn away from the river and have 6 miles of decidedly rolling terrain. A steep downhill brings you to Ausable Forks, where you soon start climbing again for Black Brook. From there you have a delightful gradual downhill that brings you to the West Branch of the Ausable River, which you follow for several easy miles. A long, gradual and very scenic climb along the West Branch, with many breaks, takes you from Wilmingon almost into Lake Placid.

Board ferry at King Street in Burlington.

0.0 Ride uphill on NY 373 west in Port Kent.

1.8 Bear left on Soper Road/Essex 17.

4.3 Turn right on Kent Street at the bottom of the hill in Keeseville.

4.4 Turn left on US 9/NY 22 south/Front Street at the flasher.

5.5 Turn right on Augar Lake Road/Essex 15.

6.2 Turn right on Dugway Road. The next few miles have sharp corners and blind crests, so stay to the right and watch for cars.

10.1 Bear right with Dugway Road for some delightful riverside riding.

10.8 Turn left uphill on Green Street.

14.4 Continue on Green Street where Grove Road is on the right, signed for Ausable Forks.

16.8 Turn right on Stickney Bridge Road at a T-intersection.

I have always enjoyed the great view here, with a small farm in front of you and mountains around the horizon.

For 82-mile ride: *Turn left here on North Jay Road and continue at the cues below.*

16.9 Turn right on Sheldrake Road/Essex 65.

18.0 If you're going slowly enough to enjoy it, there is a good view off to the left here.

19.5 Turn left across the one-lane bridge.

19.5+ Straight on US 9N north in Ausable Forks.

19.8 Continue straight on Golf Course Road where US 9N turns right.

19.9 Turn left on Essex 15/Silver Lake Road signed for Black Brook.
The next 2–3 miles will mostly be climbing.

20.8 Bear left with Essex 15 signed for Black Brook.

22.9 Bear left with Essex 15 signed for Black Brook.

23.9 Bear left with Haselton Road (sign after turn) signed for Wilmington.

24.0 Turn left at the T-junction onto Black Brook Road, which becomes Essex 12 (no sign).
The next couple of miles are among my favorite riding in the Adirondacks. You're going downhill through an almost magical forest on a curvy road.

30.9 Cross NY 86 with Essex 12 in Wilmington.
This makes a good spot for lunch, perhaps on the lawn of the church at the corner, or overlooking the river down the hill by the library; there are food options nearby.

32.7 Turn right on Indian Rock Road, also signed for Fox Farm Road—Whiteface Mountain is straight ahead of you after the turn.

33.6 Turn left onto NY 86 at the T-intersection.
Although you will generally climb for the next 9 miles, I always find this a very enjoyable uphill. It's quite gentle until the final pitch and has frequent views of the West Branch of the Ausable River tumbling down through a rocky gorge on your right. The road often

levels off, or even descends for brief stretches, giving you a break from the climb. There is always a rideable shoulder.

34.5 Ski Whiteface is on the right; there is a gondola ride to the summit—I believe you can also rent mountain bikes for the descent.

34.9 Wilmington Notch State Park is to the right.

35.9 The High Falls scenic area is a commercial site with a walk along the gorge.

42.0 The climb becomes steeper as you near the top, which is less than a mile ahead.

43.4 There is a view of the Olympic ski jumps to the left.

43.7 Junction with NY 73 in Lake Placid.

The main town is just ahead with the Tourism and Visitors Center on the left at the skating arena—they can assist with lodging if you don't have a reservation. The cues for today end at this junction and start here in the morning. You can do an optional loop around Silver Lake, which the town of Lake Placid is built on, before or after you check in to your lodging.

DAY 2: 65 MILES

Leaving Lake Placid you have an excellent view of the Olympic ski jumps before starting a long but gradual climb. At the top you're rewarded with some wonderful views as the road shares a narrow notch with elongated lakes, followed by a steep sustained downhill. You take a quiet side road alongside the East Branch of the Ausable River from Keene and have rolling riding for a few miles before the day's toughest climb—2 miles at a steep grade. However, this brings you to a fast 8-mile descent right into Elizabethtown. From there you have pastoral rolling riding on Essex 8 to Wadhams, then more of the same on NY 22 to Whallonsburg. From there you quickly gain a hilltop with an amazing panoramic view of the lake in front of you and the mountains behind. A descent to the lake through an avenue of trees framing Camel's Hump leads to easy lakeside riding and the ferry in Essex. Back in Vermont, pleasant riding in Charlotte takes you to Shelburne, then on to Spear Street and finally the waterfront bike path into Burlington.

Glorious riding on NY 73 along the Cascade Lakes, followed by a 5-mile downhill

0.0 Ride east on NY 73 and follow all signs for it.

1.1 There is a huge Adirondack chair on the left.

2.3 There is a dramatic view of the Olympic ski jumps to the right.

3.1 The Adirondack High Peaks area is to the right; a road leads to the well-known Adirondak Loj, a basecamp for hiking in the High Peaks region.

6.3 Ride past Mount Van Hoevenberg, the Olympic downhill area.

7.4 Top of the climb and the beginning of a beautiful descent along lakes in a narrow notch.

9.7 Start of the real descent, which is steep for the next 5 miles.

14.4 Turn right on Hulls Falls Road/Essex 69 in Keene just after crossing the bridge—this road has some climbing but is very attractive.

14.9 The East Branch of the Ausable River is in a gorge to the right.

16.9 Turn left on NY 73 west at a T-intersection (no sign).

17.4 Turn right on NY 9N south for Elizabethtown—there is a stiff 2-mile climb ahead.

19.7 Top of the climb and start of a major descent for the next 8 miles.

27.7 Turn left with NY 9N south where it joins US 9 north in Elizabethtown.

27.8 There is a park and bandstand on the left, a possible break/lunch stop.

28.1 Continue straight on US 9 north.

28.3 Turn right on Essex 8 signed for Wadhams. This is a lovely, rolling, wonderfully quiet road for cycling.

35.6 Turn left on Essex 22 at a T-intersection in Wadhams. Cross the Boquet River with a dam upstream and an old mill below.

35.6+ Good coffee is available at Merrick's Bakery around the corner to the left.

38.8 A magnificent brick structure complex is on the left.

This is the Essex County Home and Farm, also known as the Whallonsburg County Home and Infirmary, which is on the National Register of Historic Places.

39.5 Bear right on Whallons Bay Road (sign after turn) in Whallonsburg—ignore the BRIDGE CLOSED sign, as bikes can get through.

39.7 Turn right under the railroad overpass.

40.4 Turn left with Whallons Bay Road at the crossroads.

40.6 There is a great 360-degree panorama from this location that is well worth stopping and getting off your bike to savor.

41.1 Bear right with Whallons Bay Road.

41.3 Trees on the downhill create a viewsight for Camel's Hump straight ahead.

42.4 Turn left on Lake Shore Road at the lakefront.

The peninsula that you see jutting into the lake on the right at this turn is Split Rock or Split Rock Mountain, which forms a narrow point in the lake with Thompson Point across from it on the Vermont shore. This rock was often specified in treaties as a dividing line between warring factions and some sources indicate the rock marked the boundary between the tribes of the St. Lawrence and those of the Mohawk Valley. The Treaty of Utrecht, which ended Queen Anne's War in 1713, established Split Rock as the boundary between New France and New England, although France never accepted this.

45.1 Straight at the flasher in Essex.

45.1+ Turn right into the Essex ferry landing.
This ferry generally runs every half hour and Essex is a great town to explore if you have some extra time.

45.2 Ride straight on VT F5 from the Charlotte ferry landing.

45.6 Turn right with VT F5 at the crossroads.

46.6 Turn left on Lake Road.

48.3 Ride through a single-lane, covered bridge (second shortest in Vermont) with lake views and a park just past it with picnic tables, restrooms, and swimming—there may be a day-use fee.

49.9 Turn left on Greenbush Road at a T-intersection.

51.6 Turn right on Bostwick Road where Beach Road continues straight.

53.5 Turn left on US 7 north—this will have moderate to heavy traffic, but you're only on it for a bit over a mile and mostly downhill. The well-known Shelburne Museum in on the left.

54.8 Turn right on Webster Road just after the bridge.

54.9 Bear right on Webster Road (no sign) at the stop sign.

56.0 Turn left on Spear Street at the three-way stop.

58.9 Overlook Park is on the left—great views, especially late in the day!

59.7 Turn left on the bike path at a white barn just before Swift Street.
Note: You can optionally stay straight on Spear Street, then turn left on US 2 west/Main Street to downtown Burlington and the ferry terminal. Although it requires some navigation, the bike path is scenic and obviously has less (car) traffic. See the cues at bottom for the Spear Street route. You would also do this if your car is at one of the hotels near the I-89/US 2 interchange.

60.2 Very sharp right turn downhill on the bike path, after which you cross a wooden bridge, which can be dangerous when wet.

61.0 Turn right with the wide path at the bottom of the downhill.

61.1 Turn left on Swift Street with the bike path.

61.1+ Turn right with the path onto Farrell Street.

61.4 Cross Farrell Street with the path and turn right, then left at the corner.

61.7 Cross US 7 at the light to Home Avenue.

62.2 Cross the RR tracks to Austin Drive.

62.7 Turn right on the bike path.

62.9 Ride straight on the road bordered by boulders.
There is a side path to a rocky beach on the left, with pavilions and restrooms nearby.

63.2 Bear left on the bike path where the road curves right.

63.5 Turn right on Harrison Avenue when the bike path ends.

63.7 Turn left on the bike path just before the tracks.

64.6 Note the carved white boulders along the shore at a small peninsular park.

64.9 King Street ferry landing—end of tour.

Alternate avoiding bike path

59.7 Cross Swift Street at the light.

61.9 Turn left on US 2 west/Main Street from the "rotary" at the University of Vermont campus; or, turn right on US 2 if you've parked your car at one of the motels.

62.9 Great view of the city and lake coming downhill—especially close to sunset.

63.6 Turn left on Battery Street (right for the Radisson).

63.8 King Street ferry landing—end of the tour.

83-MILE RIDE

18.4 Fast downhill into a farming valley with mountains in front of you.

21.3 Turn left on Glen Road/Essex 22 at the bridge (good pools for swimming here).

The historic covered bridge of 1857 lies next to the road and there is a sign announcing a rehabilitation project.

22.0 Turn right on Valley Road/Essex 58.

Option: *If you have a touring or hybrid bike with sturdy wheels and wide tires, there is an adventurous optional route from here that involves very rough dirt roads and even a stream crossing or two at fords. I did this once with a road bike and thoroughly enjoyed it, but will only recommend tackling it with a bike better suited to the terrain. I believe it reduces the tour by about 15 miles, but you will have rough riding for about 10 miles (where you will probably not see anyone else) with an obviously slower pace. Caution: Be particularly slow and careful on the descents, as there can be sandy spots at the bottom of them that like to grab tires. If I haven't put you off this option yet, here's the route:*

Continue on Essex 22 here and follow it to Essex 12, where you turn left and follow it to the end, where you pick up a jeep track called Luke Glen Hill Road (don't expect signs— see the map). This becomes Wells Hill Road and brings you to Essex 12 in Lewis, which you follow to Boquet where you continue on Essex 22 north to the ferry.

24.8 Turn right on Trumbull Corners Road/Essex 12 where Essex 58 ends.

25.5 Turn left on NY 9N south in Upper Jay.

31.5 Turn right on NY 73 west in Keene and then turn left immediately on Hulls Falls Road.

This is mile 14.4 on the second day of the two-day tour; add 17.1 miles to those cues for the rest of the ride.

Whitehall–Montreal
The Grand Tour

- **DISTANCE:** 500 miles over nine days (eight riding) or lesser variations.
- **TERRAIN:** A little bit of everything—actually, a lot of everything!
- **START:** Skenesborough Museum, located on Skenesborough Drive between US 4 and Saunders Street in downtown Whitehall.
- **GETTING THERE/PARKING:** From the southern New England area take I-89 or I-91 to White River Junction, then US 4 to Rutland and Whitehall. From New York City, points south or west, get to the Albany area, drive north on I-87 to NY 149 north of Glens Falls and then US 4. There is some parking at the museum itself and additional parking along Skenesborough Drive. It's suggested that you notify the Whitehall police at 518-499-1316 and let them know where your car is and how long it will be there.

This tour is the route I used for the weeklong tours that I led around the entire lake from 1998–2001 for the Charles River Wheelmen. Due to the length of the ride and the requirements of publishing, only abbreviated format cues will be provided and no maps. Also, most references other than the necessary turns have been removed. However, sections of the route are used for other tours in this book and I will refer to them where appropriate. I suggest reading the descriptions of the other tours that cover parts of this route, as there is additional information on attractions along the way that is omitted here for space reasons.

Carry good quality and reasonably large-scale maps if doing this tour. At a minimum I recommend Northern Cartographic's Lake Champlain Region map that contains the entire route except much of the riding in Quebec and the area right around Lake Placid. If you're going to Montreal I suggest getting a street map of the city, which should also show the bike routes used. The area immediately south of the St. Lawrence will be shown on a map marked Rive Sud, and the region between there and the U.S. border is Monteregie (if you wish to get detailed maps of those areas). There are also detailed county/regional maps of Vermont from Northern Cartographic and New York's Clinton and Essex County maps are produced by Jimapco.

Specific lodging places are given below, along with reasons that I chose them for my tours, but you can usually find others nearby. Initially I had planned to stay in Essex, but discovered that there wasn't a lodging there which was large enough for my group. However, I ended up being very happy that the tour stayed in Lake Placid that night instead. The two days of riding in the Adirondacks are through excellent mountain scenery and provide a contrast to the more level riding along and near the lake. The nightly stops were based on my experience of how long a riding day club cyclists prefer and also the desire to be in towns that are interesting to explore and large enough to provide a variety of dining options. However, these were supported tours, so the daily miles may be long for some riders doing this as a loaded (self-supported) tour. With a little bit of effort you can create a tour with longer or shorter daily mileages. I will also mention some possibilities for shorter versions of this tour if you don't want to spend the full week. It's possible to do a similar tour using camping, although that will require some research on your part.

Here are some options for shorter tours if you don't have a full week available or wish to ride fewer miles per day. From Middlebury you can take the Charlotte ferry to Essex and either stay there or ride on to Westport for the night. You might want to use parts of other tours in the book if you wish to add some miles. The next day would take you to Ticonderoga or even back to Whitehall if you didn't mind a long riding day. Another option is to ride north from Burlington to the Lake Champlain Islands and take the ferry from Gordon Landing to Plattsburgh before heading for Lake Placid or staying along the lake. However, this option misses some of the best lakeside riding on the north end of the lake, so I would instead recommend riding up the islands and staying in Rouses Point before heading back south.

I haven't discussed shorter tours for Canadian riders or others who might prefer to start at the northern end of the lake, but you can also modify the route to fit your schedule or riding tastes. If you are initially riding south you could bypass Whitehall via the Ticonderoga ferry unless you really want to ride around the entire lake. With a southern start the first and last days are short, partly to allow for driving to or from the start that day, but also because that's how it works out with overnights in Middlebury and Ti. If you don't start your tour from Whitehall you don't miss much by bypassing it.

Legend for Cues

R Right turn

L Left turn

RT Right turn at T-junction

LT Left turn at T-junction

BR Bear Right

BL Bear Left

QR Quick Right (< .1 mile)

QL Quick Left (< .1 mile)

X Cross

S Straight

NS No sign (at intersection)

DAY 1

- **DISTANCE:** 48 miles.
- **START:** Skenesborough Museum in Whitehall.
- **DESTINATION:** Middlebury, Vermont.

Leaving Whitehall you soon encounter rolling hills as you cross the Poultney River into Vermont. You take VT 22A for 12 easy miles, although this road can have moderate traffic. You turn off 22A and soon have your first views of Lake Champlain and Fort Ticonderoga (where you'll be riding in a week!) with the southern Adirondacks in the distance. You turn back inland and follow scenic roads to Middlebury. My tours stayed at the Middlebury Inn (1-800-842-4666) because it was right in town and large enough to handle my group of 24 riders.

It isn't cheap, but an excellent buffet breakfast is included with your room. See tours 2 and 23 and the Middlebury regional introduction for other information.

0.0		Skenesborough Drive north from the museum
0.2	R	Saunders Street on gray bridge over canal
0.3	L	North Williams Street
1.0	L	Doig Street /Washington 10
1.6	R	Scotia Road with Washington 10
4.2	L	Staying on Scotia Road/Washington 10
6.7	X	Poultney River into Vermont on Book Road
8.8	RT	Main Road in West Haven
12.1	LT	VT 22A N
23.8	L	VT 73 W (Orwell .3 to right—nice village with store)
24.2	R	With VT 73 W
29.6	RT	VT 74 E where Ticonderoga ferry is to the left
34.2	LT	VT 74 E/VT 22A N
34.7	R	VT 74 E
42.1	LT	VT 30 N
43.6	BR	VT 30 N
46.4	R	Merchants Row after crossing stone bridge
46.5	S	US 7 S at intersection—continue uphill
46.6		Court Street at light at top of hill

The entrance to the Middlebury Inn is just to your left; if you turn right with US 7 S, the Marriott is about a mile down the road, with two motels a couple of miles farther south on US 7.

DAY 2

- **DISTANCE:** 65 miles
- **START:** Intersection of US 7 and VT 125 in Middlebury
- **DESTINATION:** Burlington, Vermont

Leaving Middlebury you ride due west toward the lake with the high peaks region of the Adirondacks rising directly in front of you. As you approach the lake you're rewarded with sweeping views of the Champlain Basin. You pass by the Chimney Point Bridge and follow back roads out to Basin Harbor before turning inland for Vergennes. You follow mostly quiet roads through Ferrisburgh and Charlotte, and finish by entering Burlington on a beautiful bike path along the lake that brings you right into the downtown area. My tours stayed at the lakefront Wyndham Burlington Hotel (60 Battery Street—802-658-6500) because it is the only Burlington lodging close to the downtown attractions and restaurants. The other large hotel chains are up the hill near the I-89/US 2 interchange and older motels are farther east on US 2 in the airport area. See tours 4 and 5 for more information.

0.0		Ride south on VT 125 W/VT 30 S from US 7
0.2	R	VT 125 W and ride through the Middlebury College campus
8.3	RT	VT 125/VT 22A N in Bridport
8.8	L	VT 125 W—store here
15.7	R	VT 17 E
17.8	BL	Lake Street at West Addison General Store
23.7	BR	Pease Road
24.5	LT	Jersey Street (NS)
25.2	S	In Panton where Panton Road enters R
25.6	BL	Button Bay Road
28.4	RT	Basin Harbor Road
32.8	LT	Panton Road
34.0	L	West Street
34.3	RT	Canal Street
34.4	LT	VT 22A over Otter Creek
34.6	L	Mcdonough Street at blinking light

Option: *Continue up the hill for lunch in Vergennes*

34.9	BR	Where High Street turns L

35.8	BR	Up Comfort Hill Road at bottom of hill
36.4	S	At stop sign—now on Bottsford Road
37.1	R	Little Chicago Road
38.0	L	US 7 N in Ferrisburg
39.4	L	Greenbush Road just after Rokeby Museum
43.6	R	Where Thompsons Point Road L
45.5	L	Ferry Road (NS) in Charlotte
46.5	R	Lake Road
49.6	LT	Greenbush Road
51.3	R	Bostwick Road where Beach Road S
53.2	L	US 7 at light—Moderate/heavy traffic
54.5	R	Webster Road just after bridge
54.6	BR	Webster Road at stop sign
55.6	LT	Spear Street at stop sign
59.5		Overlook Park on left—great views!
59.3	L	On bike path at white barn at light
59.8	RT	Sharply downhill on the bike path
60.6	R	With the wider path at the bottom of the hill
60.7	LT	Swift Street with the bike path
60.7+	QR	Farrell Street with the path
61.0	X	Farrell Street and turn right with the path, then left at the corner
61.3	X	US 7 at the light to Home Avenue
61.8	X	RR tracks to Austin Drive
62.3	R	On the bike path through the woods
62.5	S	On the road bordered by boulders
62.8	BL	On the bike path where the road curves right
63.1	R	Harrison Avenue when the bike path ends
63.3	L	On the bike path just before the tracks

64.5   King Street ferry landing

The Wyndham Burlington Hotel is just up Battery Street from the ferry landing.

Alternate avoiding bike path or for motels

59.3   **X**   Cross Swift Street at the light

61.4   **L**   US 2 W/Main Street from the "rotary" at the University of Vermont campus

Note: Turn right for the several large chain hotels located nearby; there are smaller, "traditional" motels farther east on US 2, however you will have to deal with traffic

62.4   Great view of the city and lake coming downhill—especially close to sunset

63.1   **L**   Battery Street (Wyndham Burlington Hotel to the right)

63.3   King Street ferry landing

DAY 3

DISTANCE: 81 miles.

START: Intersection of King Street and Battery Street in Burlington.

DESTINATION: Saint-Jean-sur-Richelieu, Quebec.

This is the longest day of the tour, but a large majority of the riding is flat and the rest lightly rolling. However, if you should have strong headwinds, it will be a long and hard day. Ride out of Burlington across the Winooski River into the town of that name, then you quickly gain rural roads. You skirt Mallett's Bay for a short stretch and ride on mainly back roads, bringing you to the Lake Champlain shoreline near St. Albans, which you then follow most of the way to Swanton. After crossing into Quebec you have the last northbound view of the lake at Philipsburg on Missisquoi Bay, then follow flat roads through farm country to D'Iberville and Saint-Jean-sur-Richelieu. The recommended lodging is Auberge Harris (596 Rue Champlain—1-800-668-3821), where the owner is extraordinarily friendly to touring cyclists. See tour 6 for more information on this area.

Note: If you stayed "uptown" on US 2, ride back to the intersection with Spear Street and turn right on East Avenue. This will bring you to Colchester Avenue near the top of the hill, about mile 1 on the cues.

0.0   North on Battery Street from King Street
(Modify for lodging other than the Wyndham Burlington)

0.4   **R**   Pearl Street (becomes Colchester)

1.8   **S**   Through lights at bottom of hill and cross the bridge

2.0   **L**   W. Allen Street at the light

2.1   **R**   Malletts Bay Avenue

4.6   **R**   Lavigne Road

5.2   **LT** Blakely Road

5.4   **R**   Williams Road

6.5   **RT** Lakeshore Drive

8.6   **X**   US 2/US 7 to the left

8.7   **RT** US 2A

9.5   **L**   East Road

11.6 **BR** Farnsworth Road at fork with Middle Road

12.2 **X**   One-lane RR underpass with caution

16.7 **L**   Westford Road in Milton

17.3 **RT** US 7N—moderate traffic

18.1 **L**   Lake Road uphill at store

18.6 **BL** with Lake Road

23.8 **S**   Stonebridge Road where Lake turns left downhill

25.0 **L**   Georgia Middle Road

25.3 **S**   Georgia Middle Road

27.7 **BL** Polly Hubbard Road

28.7 **RT** Georgia Shore Road

30.3 **L**   Georgia Shore Road

32.3 **L**   Georgia Shore Road at 5 corners along lake

32.6 **S**   VT 36 where it enters right—stores here

Cyclists enjoying a relaxed lunch on their way to Montreal

32.9		St. Albans Bay town park on left—restrooms in pavilion
43.2	LT	VT 36/S. River Street
43.2+	R	VT 78 E across Missisquoi River into Swanton
43.4		Swanton town green—possible lunch stop
43.5	S	US 7 N
43.7	L	US 7 N for Montreal
50.3	L	I-89 for border crossing—sign for Canada
51.0	L	Border—Canadian Customs
51.7	L	Smith Street
52.6	LT	Montgomery—signed for Philipsburg
52.7	R	Avenue Champlain (forced)
54.5	L	Quebec 133—moderate and fast traffic, but wide shoulder
56.7	L	Ch. Du Moulin
59.0	L	Quebec 133

59.2	**R**	Rg des Rivieres
63.0	**LT**	Grande Ligne/Principal
64.4	**R**	St. Edouard
66.6	**LT**	Rang Kempt
70.5	**X**	Quebec 227
75.7	**LT**	Quebec 104—moderate traffic
77.7	**LT**	Boulevard D'Iberville at light
77.7+	**QR**	9e Avenue after track
78.4	**LT**	1 Rue
78.6	**R**	onto bridge—use sidewalk on left side of bridge (right is for peds)
79.0	**R**	Richelieu at light
80.5	**L**	Auberge Harris

Note: If you want to get some Canadian cash, turn left on Quay just at the end of the bridge and make the next two right turns onto Richelieu. On the right is Banque Royale with an ATM. Then continue straight on Richelieu.

DAY 4

DISTANCE: 31 miles.

START: Auberge Harris, Saint-Jean-sur-Richelieu.

DESTINATION: Montreal, Quebec.

This is a very direct route to Montreal that uses bike paths, but also spends some time on moderately busy urban streets. Since check-in time for hotels is usually 3 PM, you may choose to make a late departure. The other option is to leave your panniers at your Montreal lodging and explore the city by bike until your room is ready. This route brings you to the corner of Rue Guy and Boulevard Rene Lavesque in Montreal. I recommend the Nouvel Hotel (1740 Boulevard Rene Lavesque—1-800-363-6063), which is a couple of blocks to the left from this intersection. The Montreal youth hostel (1030 Rue Mackay—514-843-3317) is a block to the right on Mackay. This is a very pleasant hostel with two-person rooms available, but do book well in advance.

0.0	L	Champlain from Auberge Harris
1.7	R	St. Therese over bridge
1.9	BL	On bike path
4.5	L	Over bridge (bike path continues right unpaved)

(You can follow this to mile 10.3 if you wish)

4.5+	RT	Quebec 223
6.4	X	One-lane bridge—cross bike path
8.9	X	Quebec 112
9.0	R	Richelieu
9.2		Dramatic falls and rapids, especially in spring
9.8	L	(Optionally visit park and fort ahead)
9.9	RT	Bourgogne
10.3		Bike path joins road at the canal locks
10.7	BL	Chemin Salaberry at light
10.8	X	Quebec 112 at light
11.2	X	Boulevard Brassard
11.8	BR	With Salaberry
14.7	R	Grande Allee over bridge
15.0	S	Grand Allee
20.1	X	Boulevard Gaetan-Boucher at light
21.0	S	Grand Allee where the main road **BL**
22.6	X	Boulevard Edouard at light
22.9	L	Montcalm
23.1	X	Quebec 134/Taschereau at light
23.2	L	Jeannette
23.9	RT	Victoria
23.9+	QL	Rothesay (NS)

24.1   **LT**   Arran

24.1+   **R**   Rivermere

24.7   **X**   Riverside to bike path ramp

24.8   **S**   Up bike ramp crossing the X-way and the seaway—Use caution at gates!

25.1   **R**   (U-turn) on bike path under bridge

25.8   **S**   Join Formula 1 racetrack after crossing onto Ile Notre-Dame

26.5   **R**   For bike ramp up to bridge after crossing under the bridge on race-track

Continue with bike path on the bridges over the St. Lawrence—there are excellent views of the Montreal skyline and Mont Royal itself as you ride by the old port area.

28.4   **R**   With bike path at X-way overhead

28.9   **X**   Mill Street under X-way with bike path—stay on left side of the canal signed for Lachine

29.7   **R**   Rue des Seigneurs at first road bridge

30.0   **R**   Rue Notre Dame after 3 short blocks

30.2   **L**   Rue Guy at light. Short and steep hill here

30.6   Boulevard Rene Levesque at top of hill—Nouvel Hotel left, hostel on Mackay to the right

DAY 6

DISTANCE: 73 or 84 miles.

START: Corner of Rue Guy and Boulevard Rene Levesque in Montreal.

DESTINATION: Plattsburgh, New York.

Our route is the one used on my annual Memorial Day Dash to Montreal tour. You leave Montreal on bike paths for most of the first 15 miles. Then follow back roads in Quebec to the border crossing in Champlain, New York. Shortly after this you gain distant views over the Lake Champlain Basin while riding on quiet roads in farm country, then cruise through apple orchards before cycling next to the lake. The recommended lodging is the Super 8 Motel—Plattsburgh (7129

Route 9—518-562-8888). This is located a bit more than 2 miles from the business district of the city. There are some motels along the lake about a mile farther south, but most if not all of these have been converted to temporary housing and they can't be recommended. There are a half-dozen large hotels near Exit 37 of I-87 where it crosses NY 3, but this is a busy strip area and not friendly for cyclists. For dinner I suggest cycling (or taking a taxi) to Irises Café and Wine Bar in the old section of town. See tour 14 for more information.

Option: Those wishing to cycle the beautiful Lake Champlain Islands can do so, adding some 11 miles to their day's ride. The turnoff for this is about mile 42, so you can make the decision based on the weather and how you're feeling at that point.

0.0		Ride NE on Rene Levesque toward downtown
0.4	R	Peel
1.1	L	Wellington
1.4	R	Prince
1.5	L	Then cross the blue-arched bridge to Mill
1.9	L	On bike path under the expressway
2.4	L	With bike path
4.6	BL	On bike ramp down to Ile Notre Dame
4.8	L	On grand prix race course
5.5	BR	On bike path off racecourse
6.2	L	Up to bike path crossing seaway
6.5	R	Bike path along Rue Riverside
7.7	R	Boulevard Simard
7.9	L	On bike path along the river

Note: public restroom soon on L

9.5	L	Boulevard Rome under expressway
9.9	R	On bike path in greenbelt; straight at playground
11.5	X	Matte—special bike path light

12.2	**RT**	With the bike path
12.7	**S**	A bike path enters L
13.1	**X**	Road with bike path
13.4	**L**	Longtin with bike path at circle
13.5	**R**	Desjardins with bike path
13.9	**R**	Salaberry with bike path
15.1	**L**	Montcalm Sud
16.8	**L**	Jean Leman signed for Quebec 30
17.6	**S**	At overpass of Quebec 30
18.9	**L**	St. Andre (forced)
20.6	**L**	Montee Monette signed for St. Philippe
21.6	**S**	Montee Monette in St. Philippe—restroom in cafe
21.7	**R**	St. Marc
25.2	**L**	Quebec 217 S at crossroads
26.9	**R**	St. Jacques at sign for St. Edouard
26.9+	**QL**	St. Phillippe
29.1	**RT**	Langevin
29.2	**L**	du Coteau
33.4	**X**	Quebec 219/221—restaurant and store here
41.8	**L**	**For 84-mile ride:** Montee DuPuis for the Lake Champlain Islands continue below
41.8	**S**	For 73-mile ride
42.7	**X**	Quebec 202
45.9	**L**	Rue Guay
48.0	**R**	Quebec 221 S
49.0		Border—U.S. Customs
50.4	**X**	Prospect

51.0   **X**   US 9 to Mason Road

51.8   **BR**   with main road

53.9   **RT**   NY 9B S

54.1   **L**   Lake Shore Road

58.0   **BL**   Shore Road where N. Farm Road R

64.6   Monty Bay Marina L—small store + deck

67.3   **R**   With main road at entrance to Point Au Roche State Park

69.1   **L**   US 9 S—moderate traffic

72.9   **R**   Super 8 Motel—Plattsburgh

84-mile ride

41.8   **L**   Montee DuPuis

42.9   **X**   St. Claude

44.9   **RT**   Quebec 221 S (NS) in Lacolle

44.9+ **QL**   Mtee Van Vliet—railroad underpass just ahead

45.9   **BR**   Mtee Bowman at fork

46.7   **RT**   Quebec 223 S at blockhouse

46.8   **L**   Quebec 202 E and cross bridge over Richelieu River

48.5   **R**   Quebec 225 S in Noyan

52.4   Border—U.S. Customs

54.0   **LT**   US 2 S

54.4   Alburg—several stores here

55.6   **R**   Shore Road where US 2 curves left

60.2   **BL**   Where VT 129 crosses causeway R

Option: *R on VT 129 for Isle La Motte (see tour 13)*

62.9   **RT**   US 2

68.8   Restroom at Hero's Welcome store in North Hero

76.9   **R**   VT 314 at sign for ferry to NY

80.1   **R**   Gordon Landing ferry landing

80.2   **L**   leaving ferry landing in NY

84.1   **R**   US 9 N at light

84.1+   **QL**   Super 8 Motel

DAY 7

DISTANCE: 51 or 58 miles.

START: Super 8 Motel, Plattsburgh, New York.

DESTINATION: Lake Placid, New York.

For breakfast, I recommend the Cumberland Café in downtown Plattsburgh, which is on your route. There is an optional detour after breakfast to visit a large and varied collection of outdoor sculpture on the SUNY campus (see tour 16). You have generally easy riding as you leave town and slowly start gaining elevation approaching the mountains to the southwest. Ride into the Adirondacks with the route gently gaining elevation through wooded areas. The long route is much hillier than the short route, although it also provides more spectacular views of the region. After Wilmington you have about a 10-mile gradual climb along the West Branch of the Ausable River. The cues end at the intersection of NY 86 and NY 73 in Lake Placid. There are many lodging options, although you might have a hard time without reservations. I recommend checking with the Lake Placid/Essex County Convention and Visitors Bureau at 216 Main Street (1-800-44PLACID), as they can check the status of most rooms in town on their system. See tour 24 for more information.

0.0   **R**   US 9 S

0.1   **S**   US 9 S at light

1.3   **L**   Cumberland Avenue at light

2.4   **R**   Bridge Street

2.4+   **LT**   Margaret—Cumberland Café is on the right

2.6   **X**   Broad to Pine Street at light

Option: *R to see sculpture on SUNY campus*

2.9	L	Pine Street along the river
3.5	L	S. Catherine/NY 22 S
4.4	R	Peru/NY 22 S at blinker
4.5	R	NY 22 S
8.0	S	**For 58-mile ride:** continued below.
8.0	R	**For 51-mile ride:** Salmon River Road at sign for Schuyler Falls
11.8	LT	NY 22 B S
11.9	R	Norrisville Road signed for Macomb State Park
16.4	RT	Peasleeville Road
22.5	BL	In Peasleeville
30.9	R	St. Matthews Road
31.7	RT	Clinton 33 (NS)
31.9	BL	Bear left with Haselton Road signed for Wilmington
32.0	LT	Black Brook Road (NS) becomes Essex 12
38.5	X	Essex 86 with Essex 12 in Wilmington—possible lunch stop—restroom at library
40.4	R	Fox Farm Road
41.2	LT	Essex 86—start of gradual climb along Ausable River
50.3		Top of climb
51.3		NY 73—the main part of Lake Placid is straight ahead and the Visitors Bureau will be on the left at the skating arenas

58-mile ride

12.7	LT	NY 22 S in Peru
18.6	S	Pleasant Street in Keeseville at light
18.8	R	Front Street/US 9 S/NY 22 S in Keeseville
19.9	R	Augar Lake Road/Essex 15
20.6	R	Dugway road

24.5	**R**	Dugway Road at Cassidy Road
25.2	**L**	Green Street uphill
31.2	**R**	Stickney Bridge Road at North Jay Road
31.3	**R**	Sheldrake Road/Essex 65
33.9	**LT**	Across the one-lane bridge
33.9+	**S**	US 9N N in Ausable Forks
34.2	**S**	Golf Course Road—get ready for climbing
34.3	**L**	Essex 15/Silver Lake Road signed for Black Brook
35.2	**BL**	With Essex 15 signed for Black Brook
37.3	**BL**	With Essex 15 signed for Black Brook
38.3	**BL**	Bear left with Haselton Road signed for Wilmington

This is mile 31.9 on main route; continue with those cues

DAY 8

DISTANCE: 57 or 62 miles.

START: Intersection of NY 86 and NY 73 in Lake Placid.

DESTINATION: Ticonderoga, New York.

Leaving Lake Placid you have a dramatic view of the Olympic ski jumps before starting a long but gradual climb. At the top you're rewarded with some wonderful views as the road shares a narrow notch with elongated lakes, followed by a steep sustained downhill. You take a delightful side road alongside the East Branch of the Ausable River from Keene and have rolling riding for a few miles before the day's toughest climb—2 miles at a steep grade. There are a couple of optional side trips in Ticonderoga, including the famous fort, so you might wish to get into town early to do some exploring—see the Ticonderoga regional introduction for information on these options. There are about a half dozen motels in Ticonderoga and the cues will take you to the visitors center in town, which is near most of the lodging. See the Ti regional info and tours 21 and 22 for more info.

There is also a long option that adds 5 miles. This turns off very late in the day, so you can wait and see how you are feeling. It starts with a fairly easy and scenic climb along a stream, then visits a small historic museum in Penfield (see tour 22) and ends with a long downhill almost to Ticonderoga.

0.0		Ride east on NY 73
2.0	BR	NY 73 signed for Keene
7.4		Top of the first climb
9.7		Start of descent that is fairly steep for the next 5 miles
14.4	R	Halls Falls Road in Keene just after the bridge
16.9	RT	NY 73 E at a T-junction
18.9		Keene Valley
21.4		St. Huberts—start of steep climb
23.6		top of climb at Chapel Pond
30.0	L	Essex 6
37.7	X	Essex 70
38.0	BR	Raymond Wright Avenue (no sign) downhill after the stop
38.9	RT	Essex 7 in Mineville
41.2	L	Essex 7 at stop in Moriah Center
41.2+	S	Essex 7 with sign for Moriah Corners
49.9	X	**For 57-mile ride:** Essex 2
49.9	R	**For 62-mile ride:** Essex 2; continue below
49.9+	QR	Essex 7 after grassy triangle
50.0	L	Essex 7
50.6	X	Essex 47
54.2	RT	NY 9N S—moderate traffic
55.7	BR	NY 9NS
56.2	X	NY 74 at light
56.9		Monument Street at rotary—Tourist info booth here and motels nearby

62-mile ride

52.0	**BL**	Essex 2 at fork
52.7	**S**	Where Essex 47 joins from the left
54.1		Penfield Museum (see tour 22)
54.3	**BL**	Corduroy
57.4	**LT**	NY 74 E
61.3	**R**	NY 9NS
62.0		Monument Street at rotary—Tourist info booth here and motels nearby

DAY 9

DISTANCE: 25, 32, or 44 miles.

START: Intersection of NY 9N and Monument Street in Ticonderoga.

DESTINATION: Whitehall, New York.

I highly recommend the Hot Biscuit Diner near the circle for breakfast. There is a 26-mile direct but quite hilly route back to Whitehall using NY 22 all the way, which provides a true circumnavigation of the lake. There are two longer but flatter possibilities that involve taking the Ticonderoga ferry to Larabees Point in Vermont and riding south on VT 22A to New Haven. These will take you back over roads that you cycled on eight days earlier, which you may see as either a positive or negative thing. See tour 2 for more info.

25-mile ride

0.0		East on Montcalm Street from the circle
1.2	**R**	NY 22 at flasher
26.1	**L**	Sanders Street in Whitehall
26.1+	**QR**	Main Street
26.3		Skenesborough Museum—end of the tour

32- or 44-mile ride

0.0		East on Montcalm Street from the circle
1.2	X	NY 22 onto NY 74 E at flasher
2.0	S	Ticonderoga ferry landing
2.1	S	VT 74 Larabees Point ferry landing
2.6	R	VT 73
7.9	BL	VT 73
8.3	R	VT 22A S with moderate traffic
14.3	S	VT 144 on left—store here
22.6	X	US 4
23.5	R	West Street at church before the green in Fair Haven

For 44-mile ride: *Continue S on VT 22A here and see tour 1*

25.7	L	Carleton Road
28.8	BR	Washington 9
30.8	X	Washington 10
21.7	R	Saunders Street over bridge
31.8	L	Main Street
31.9		Skenesborough Museum—end of the tour